THE LIFE OF CHRIST IN WOODCUTS

THE LIFE OF CHRIST IN WOODCUTS

❖ JAMES ❖ REID ❖

DOVER PUBLICATIONS, INC.
Mineola, New York

Bibliographical Note

This Dover edition, first published in 2009, is an unabridged republication of the work originally published by Farrar & Rinehart, Inc., New York, in 1930.

Library of Congress Cataloging-in-Publication Data

Reid, James, 1907–1989.
The life of Christ in woodcuts / James Reid.
p. cm.
Originally published: New York : Farrar & Rinehart, 1930.
ISBN-13: 978-0-486-46884-6
ISBN-10: 0-486-46884-4
1. Jesus Christ—Art. 2. Jesus Christ—Biography. I. Title.

NE1112.R45A4 2009
769.92—dc22

2008037663

Manufactured in the United States of America
Dover Publications, Inc., 31 East 2nd Street, Mineola, N.Y. 11501

To ALYSE
and alyse

THE INFANT

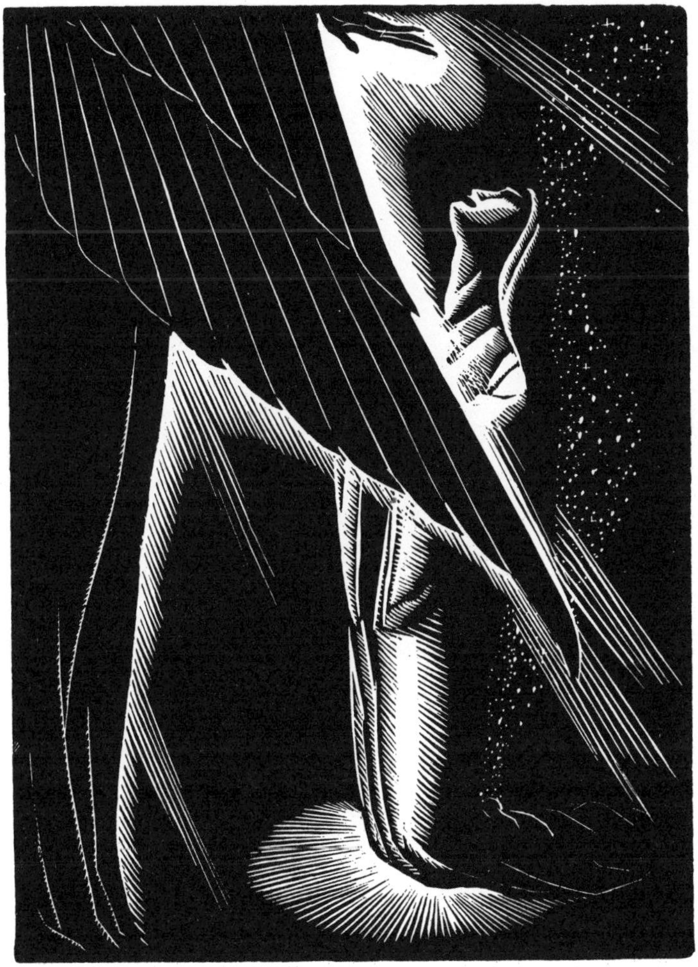

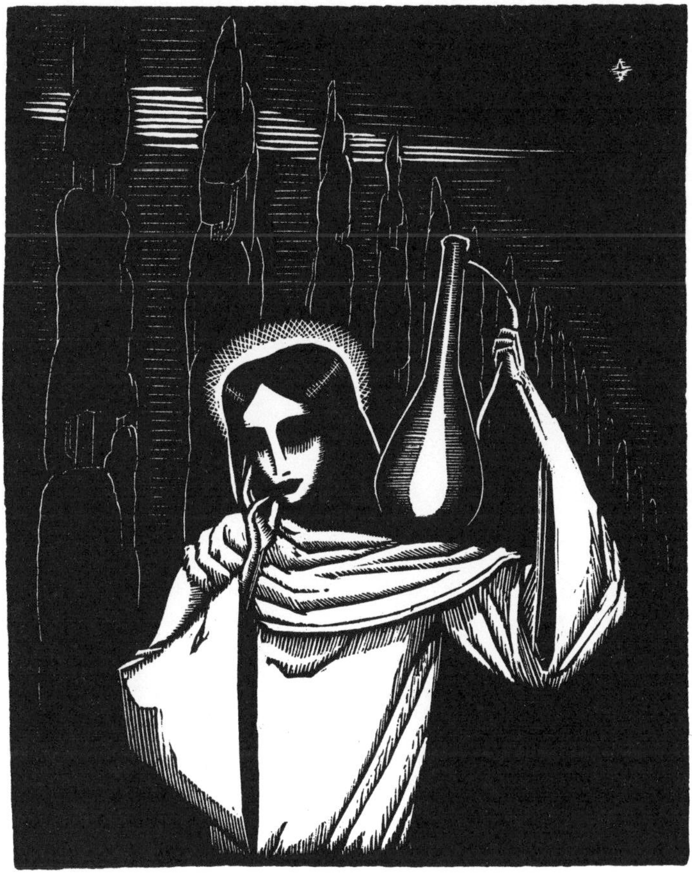

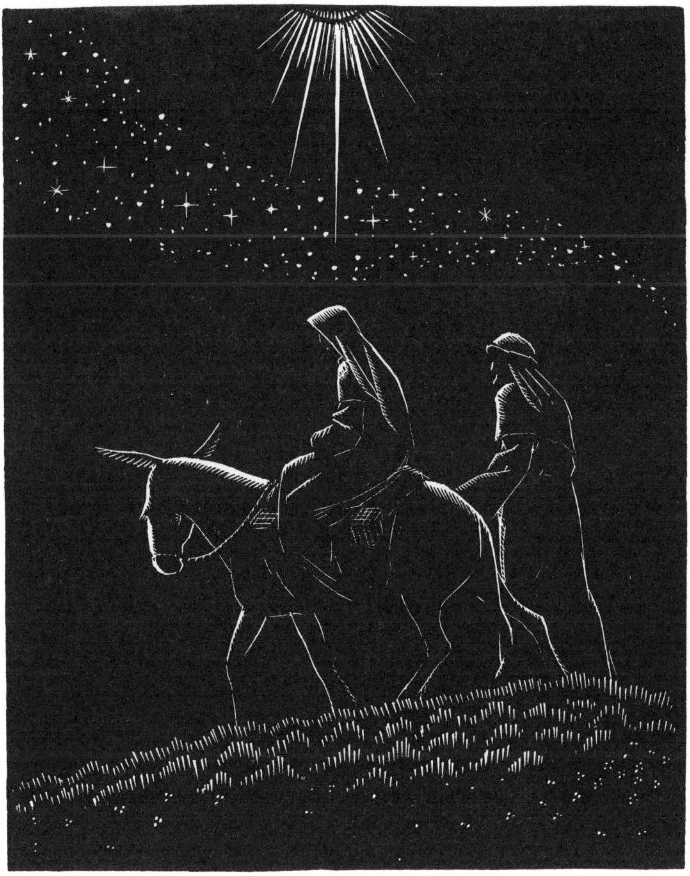

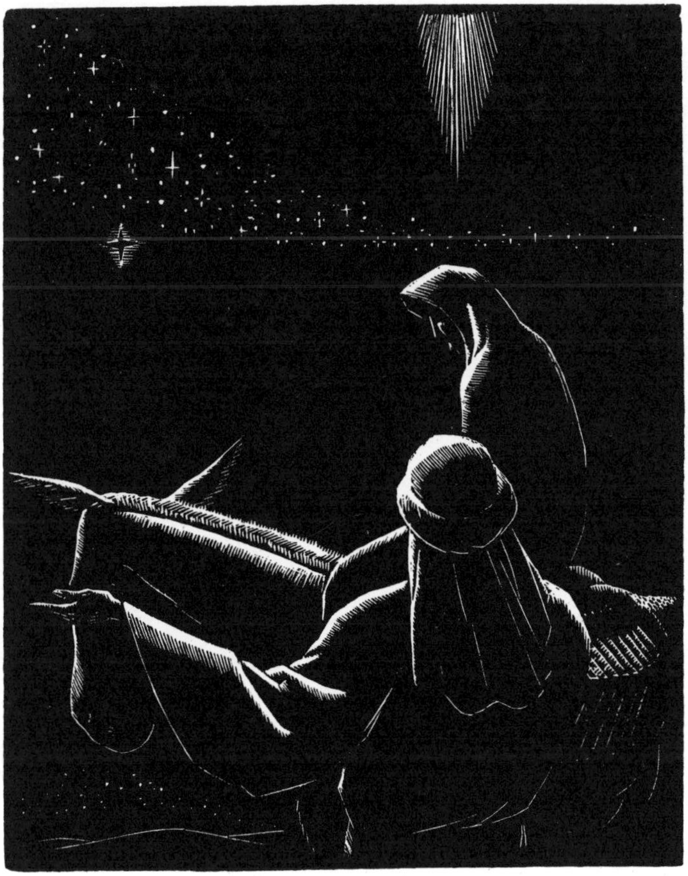

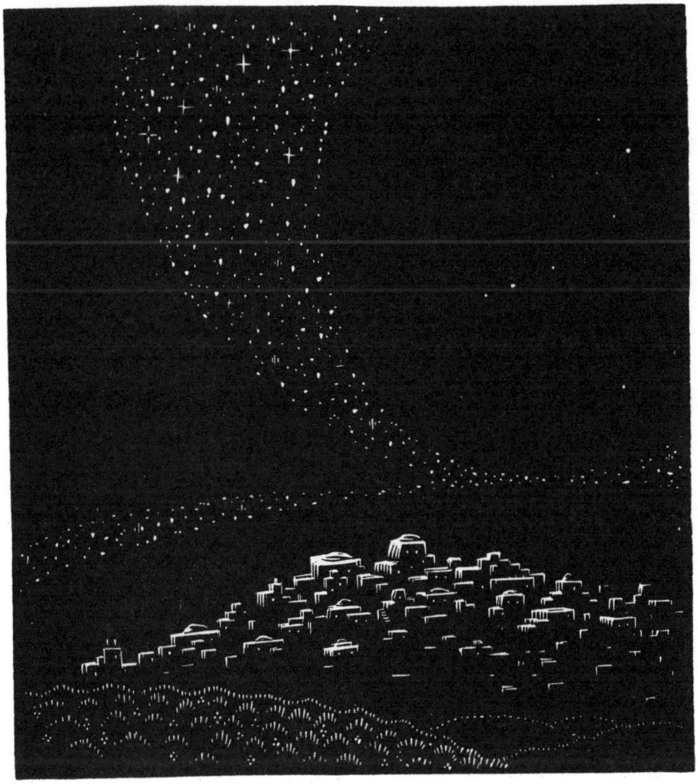

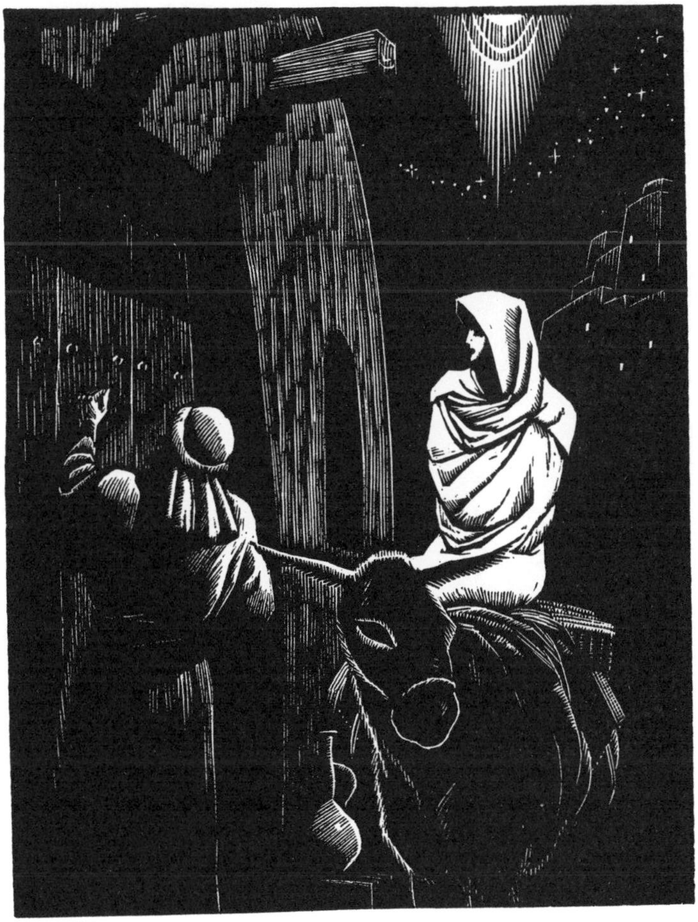

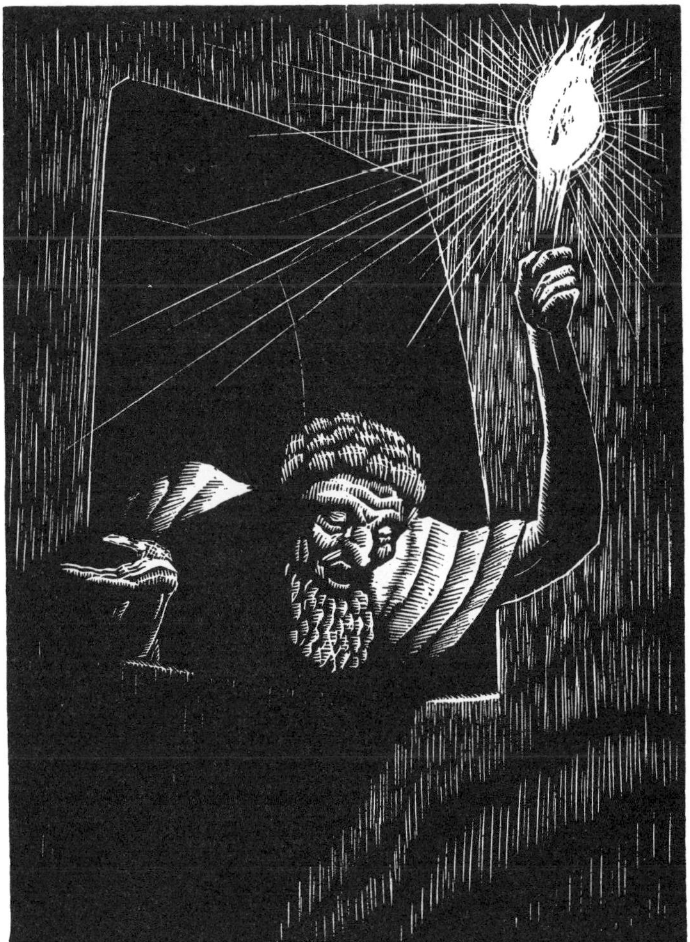

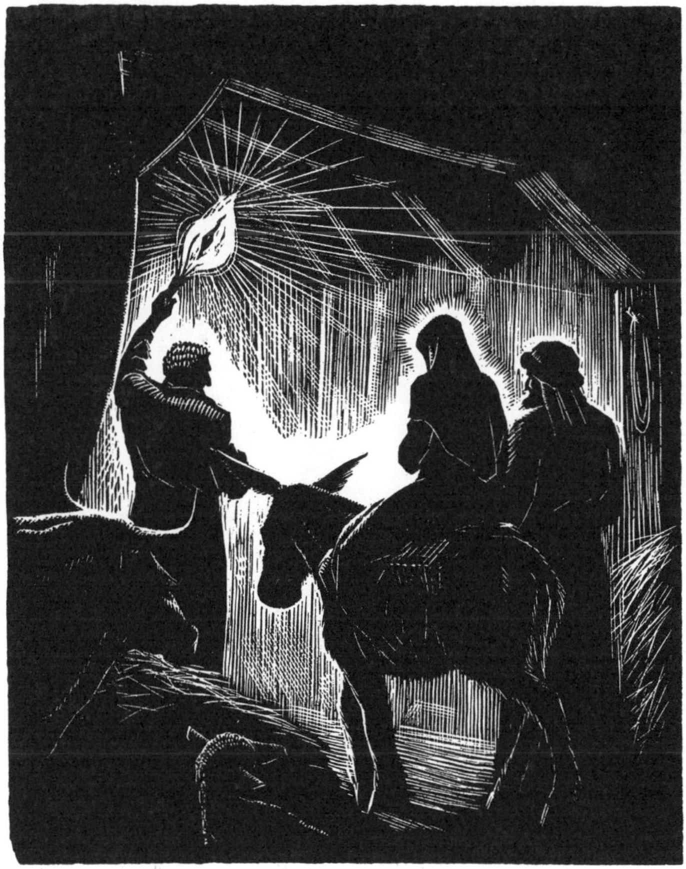

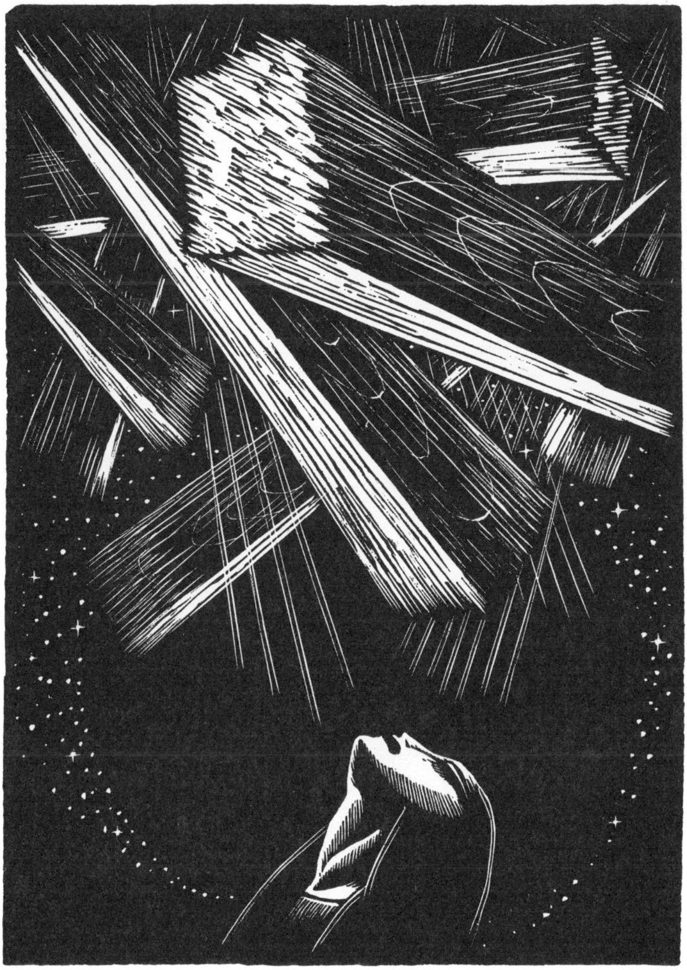

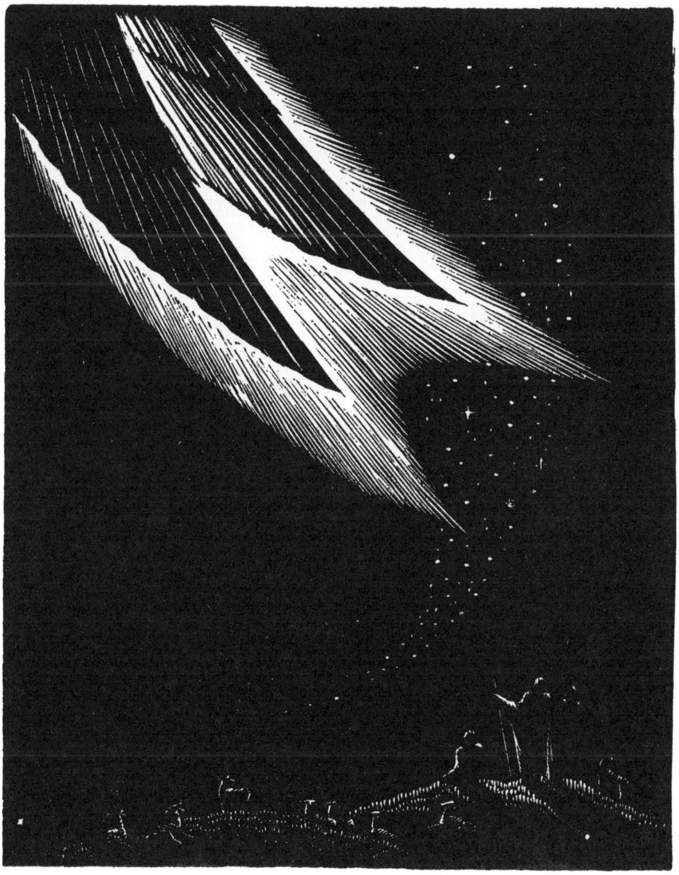

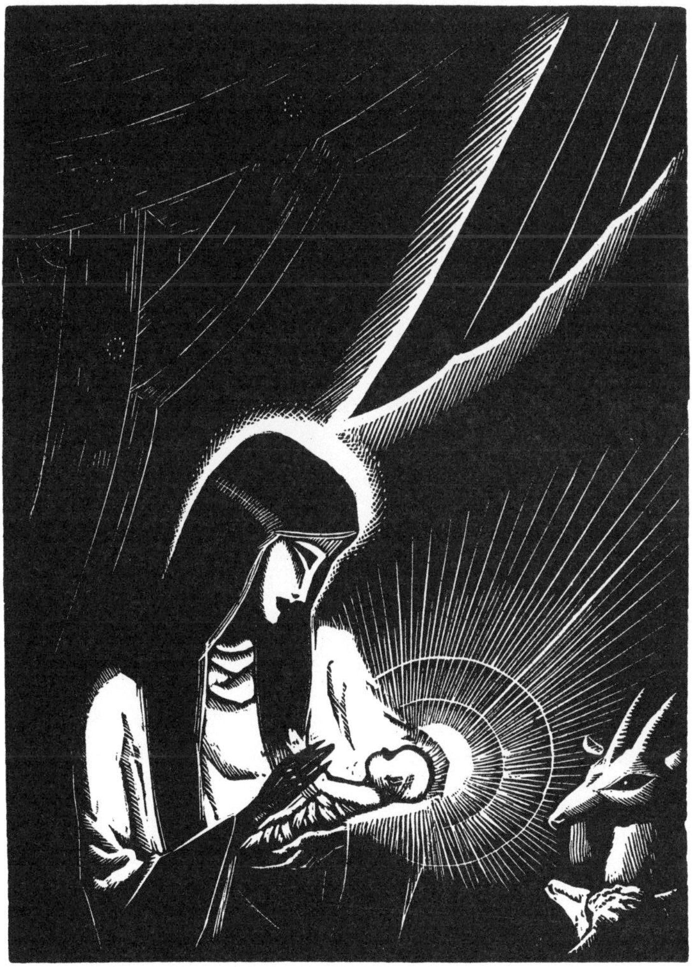

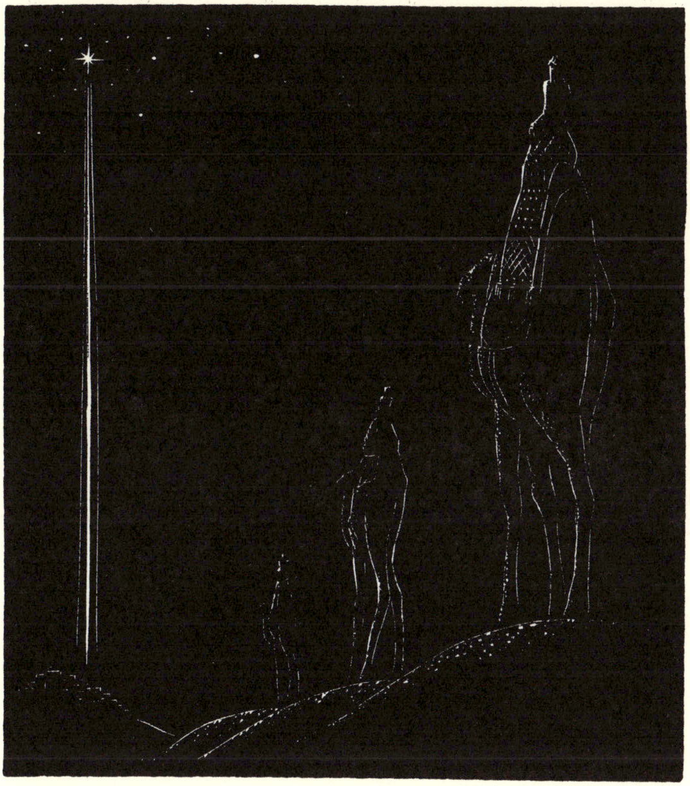

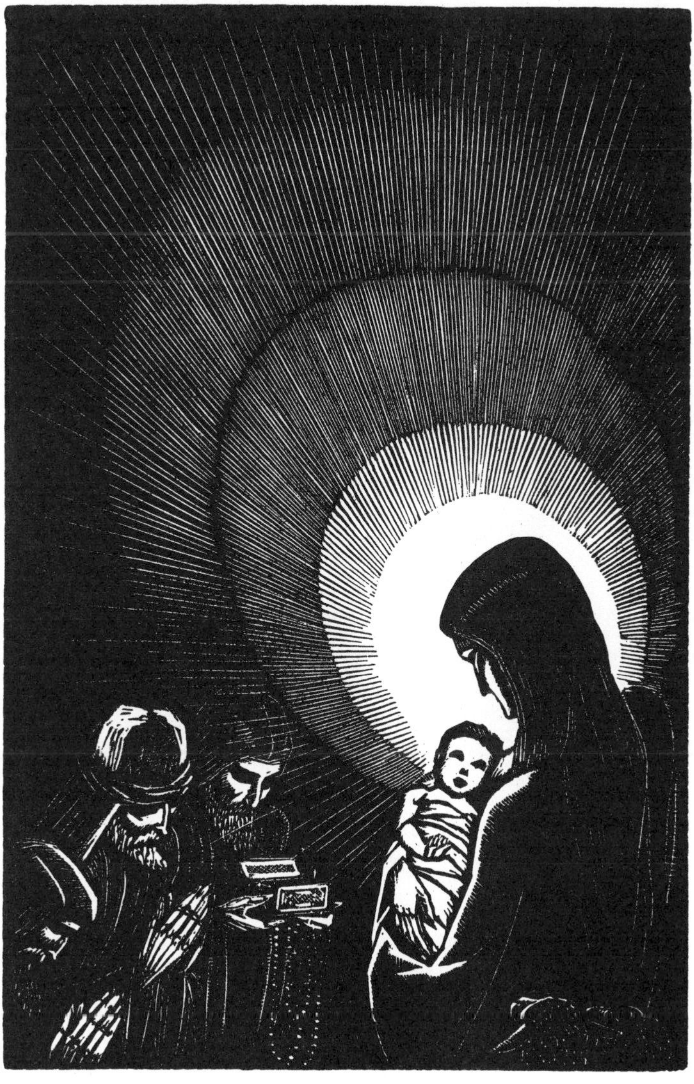

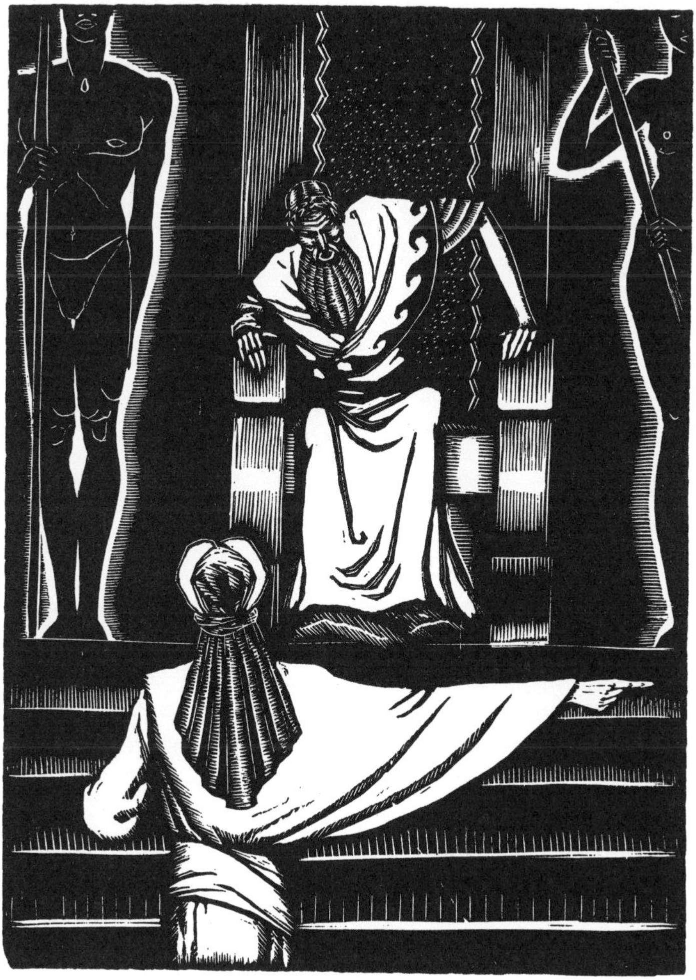

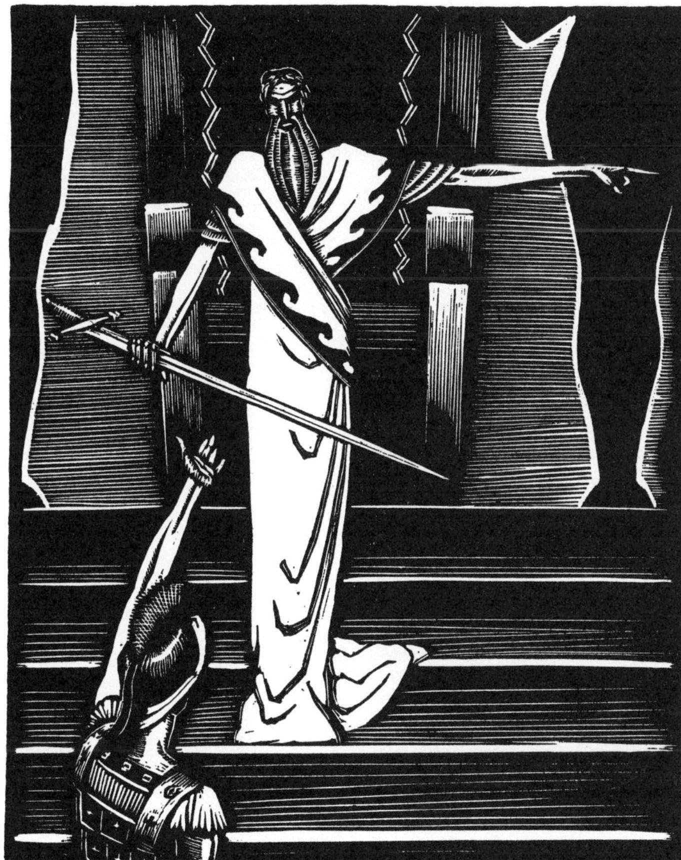

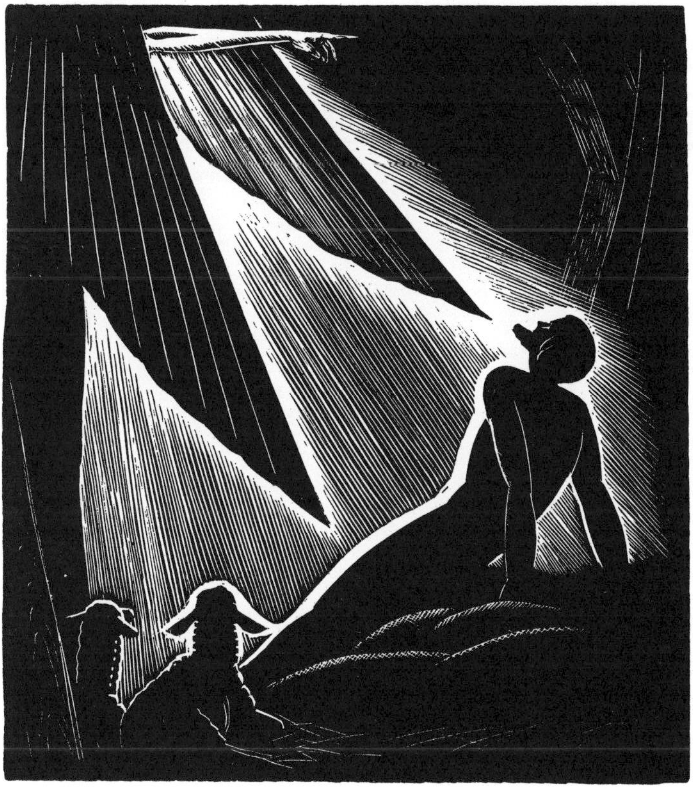

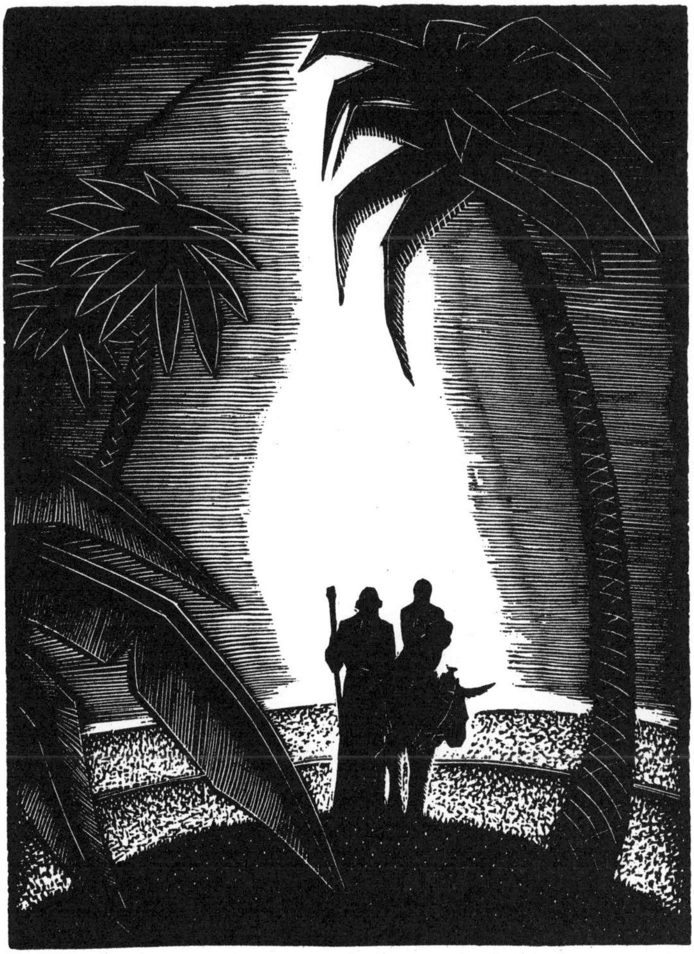

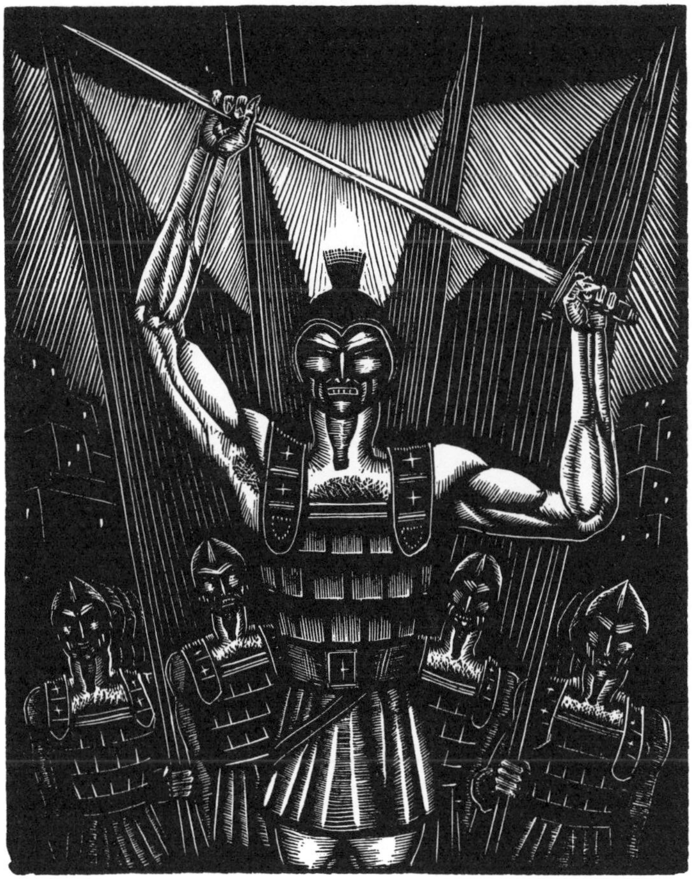

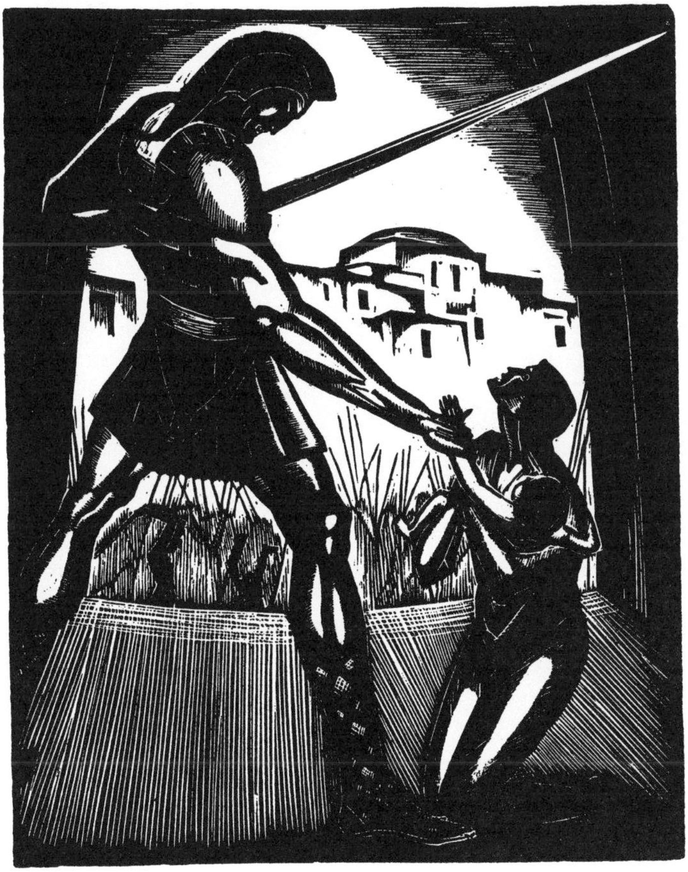

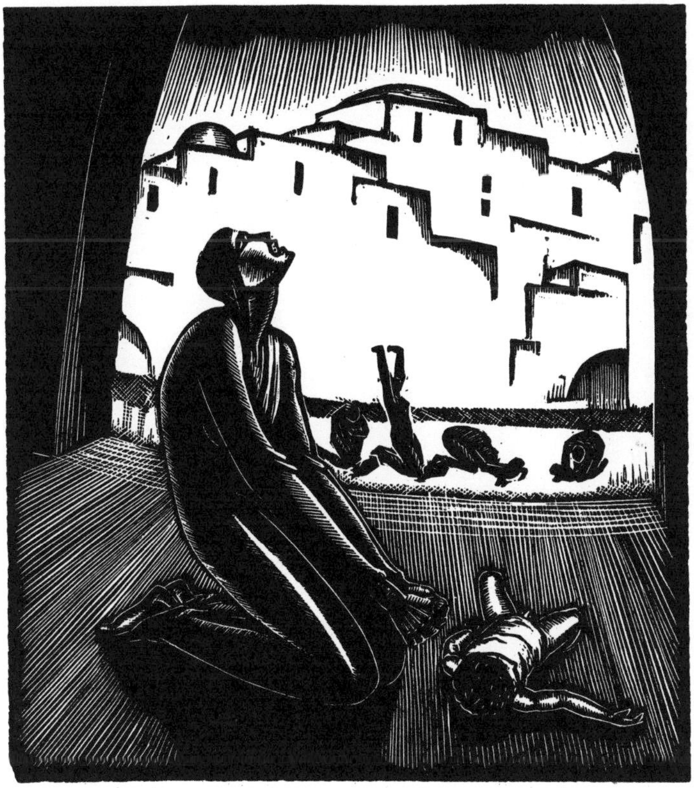

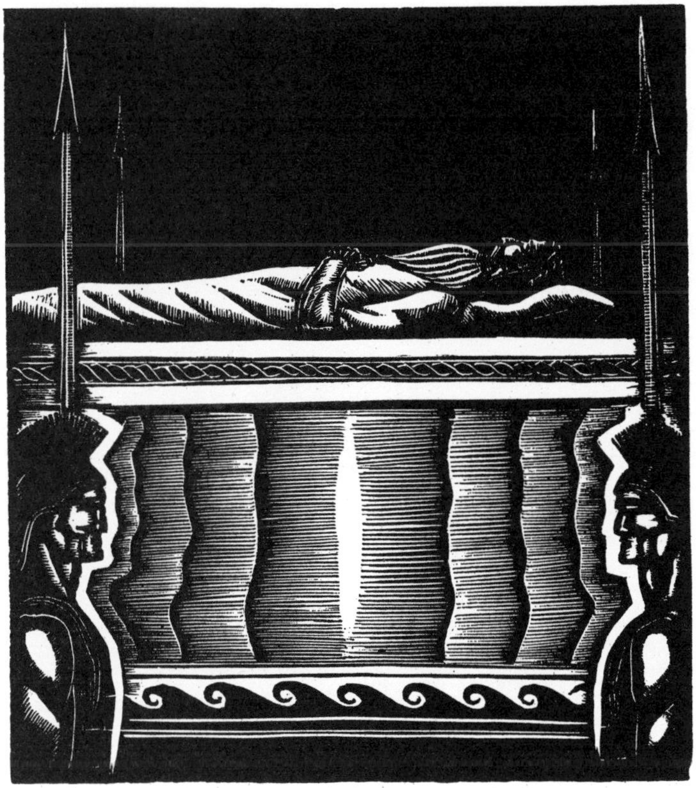

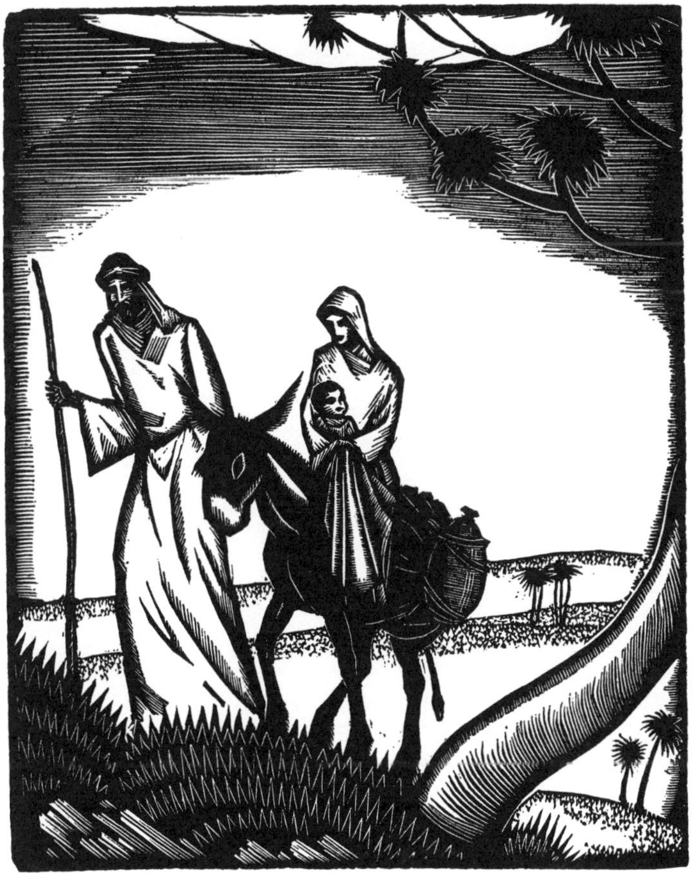

THE BOY

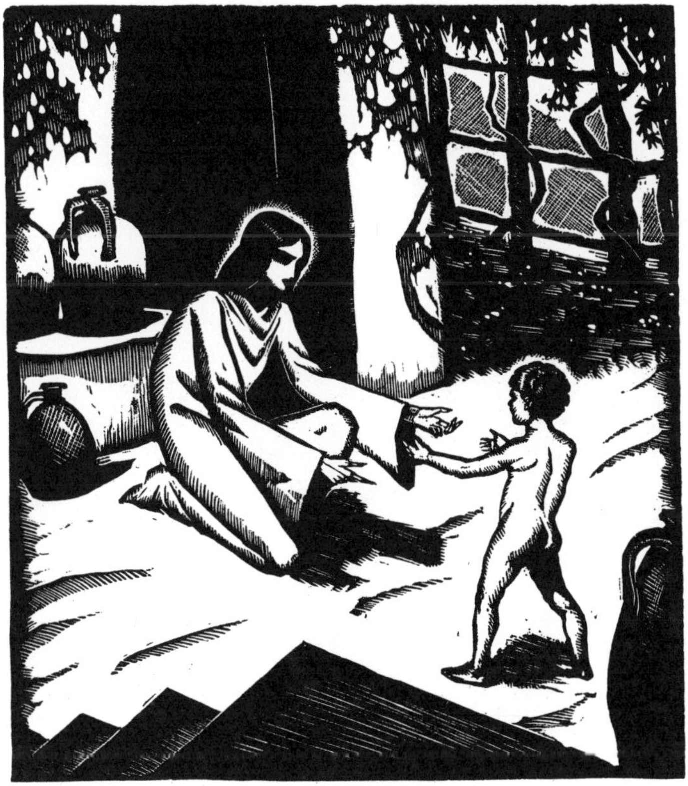

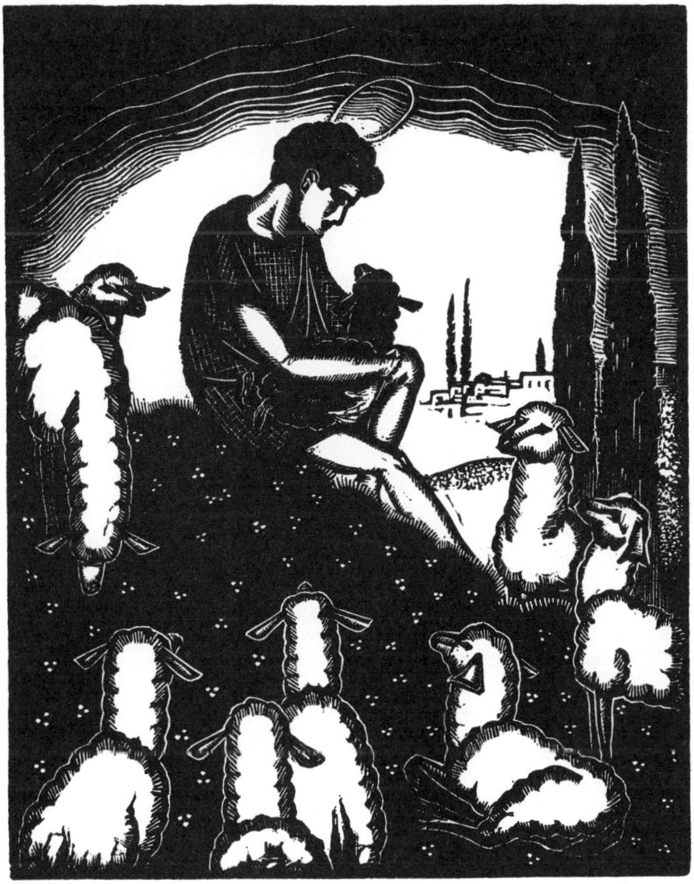

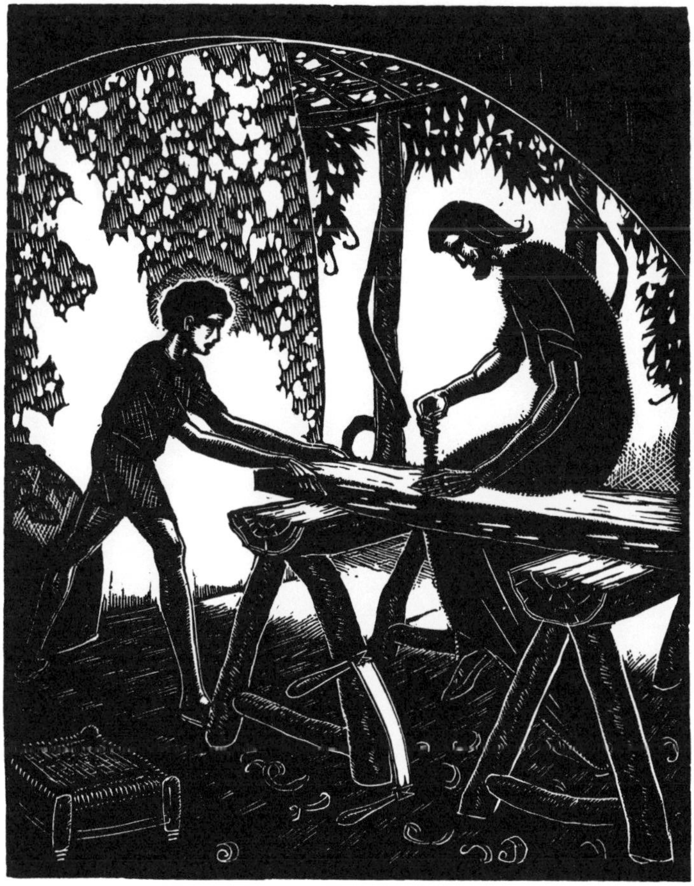

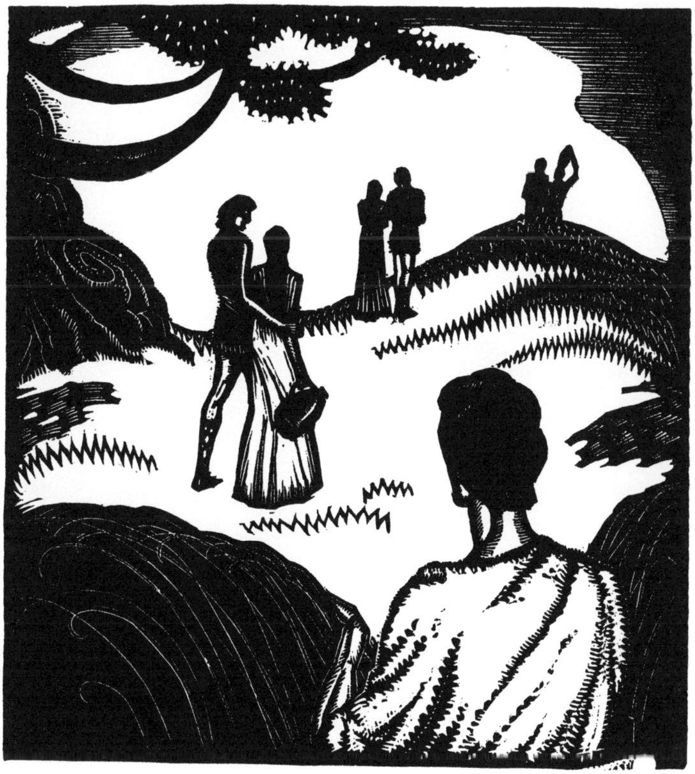

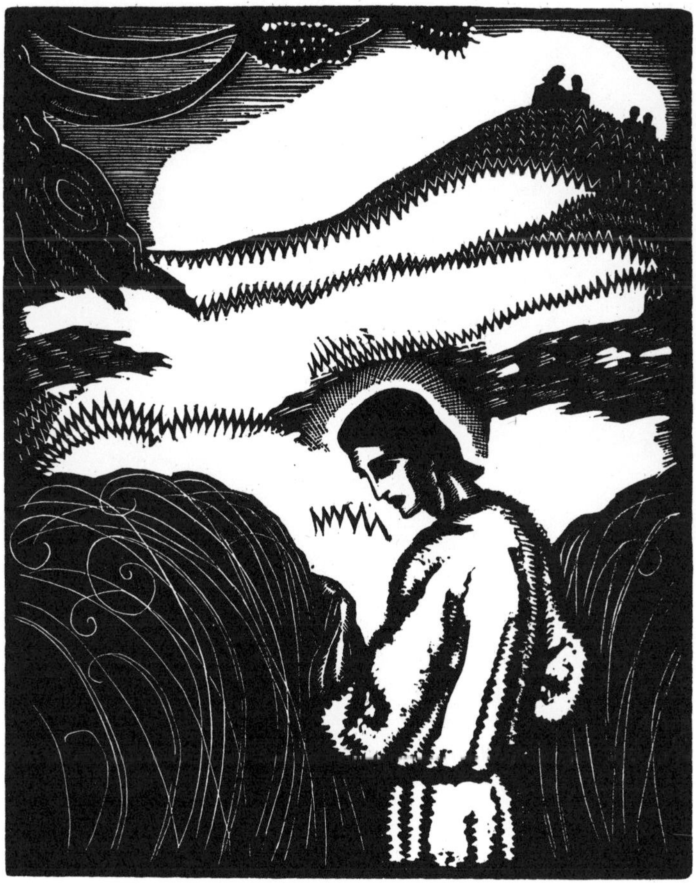

THE SON OF GOD

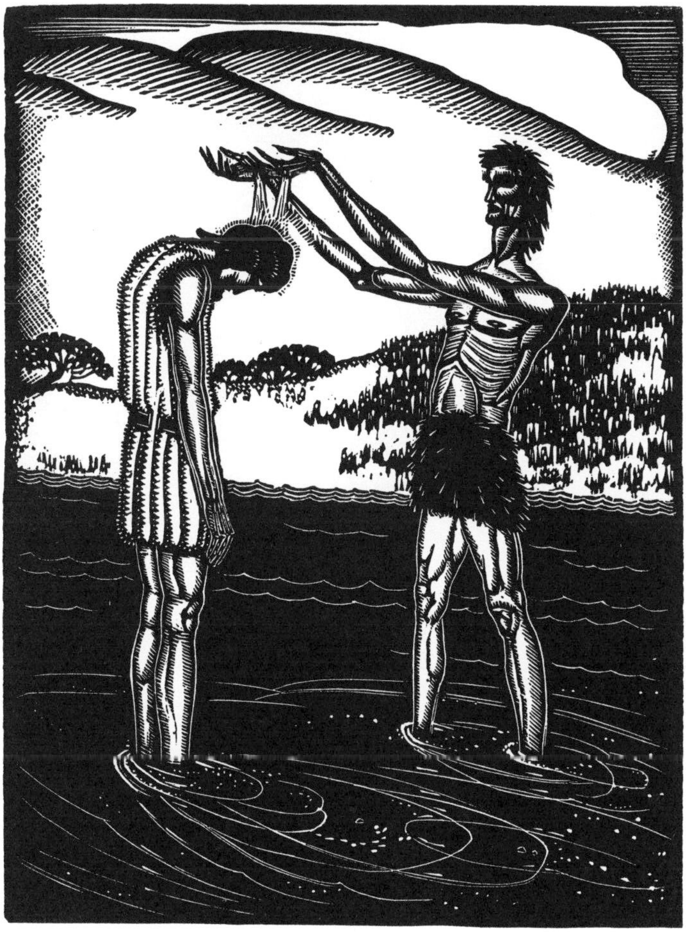

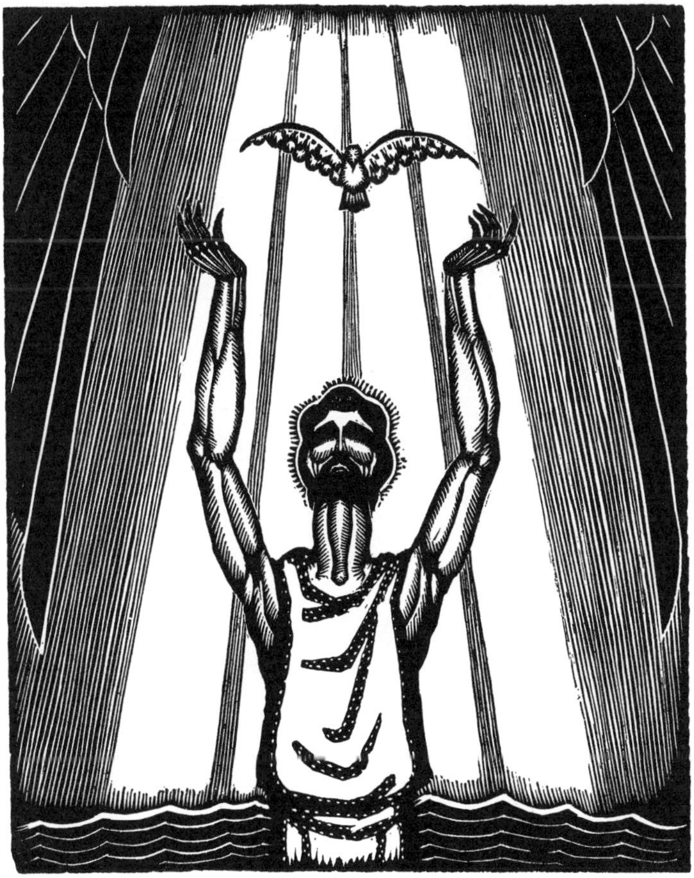

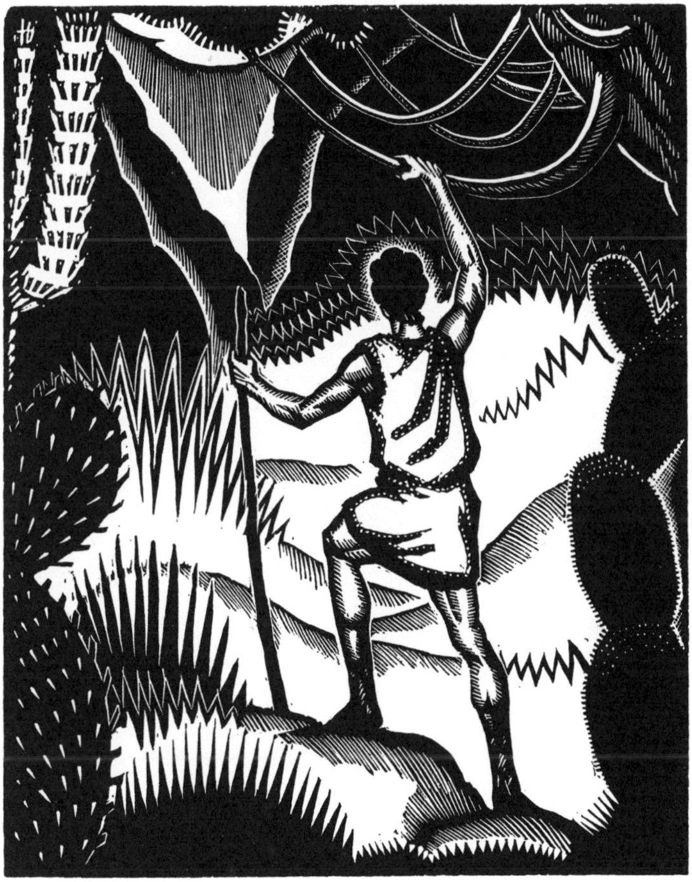

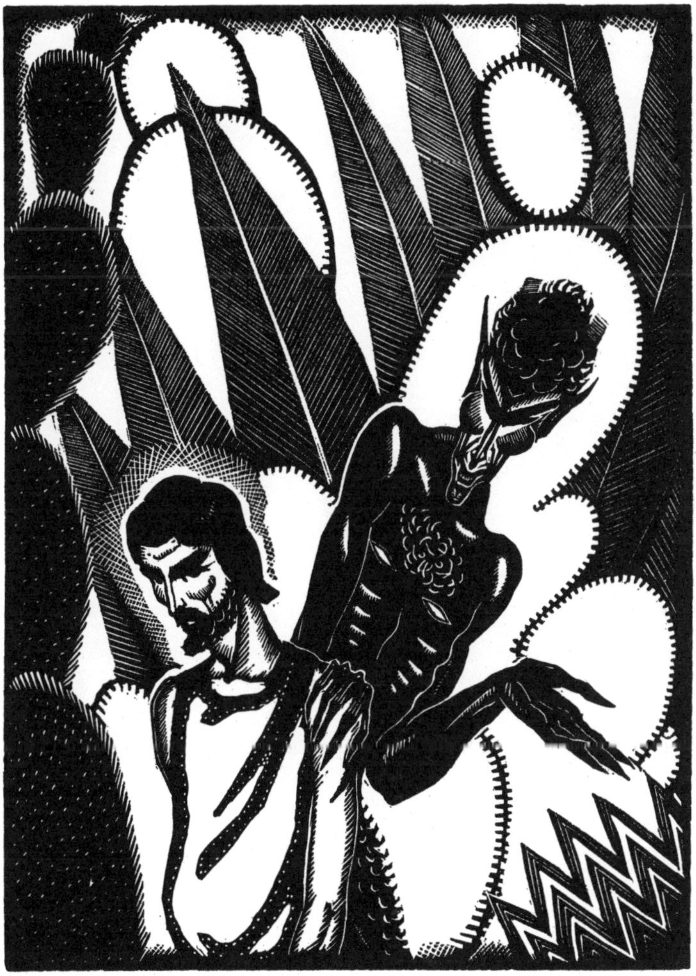

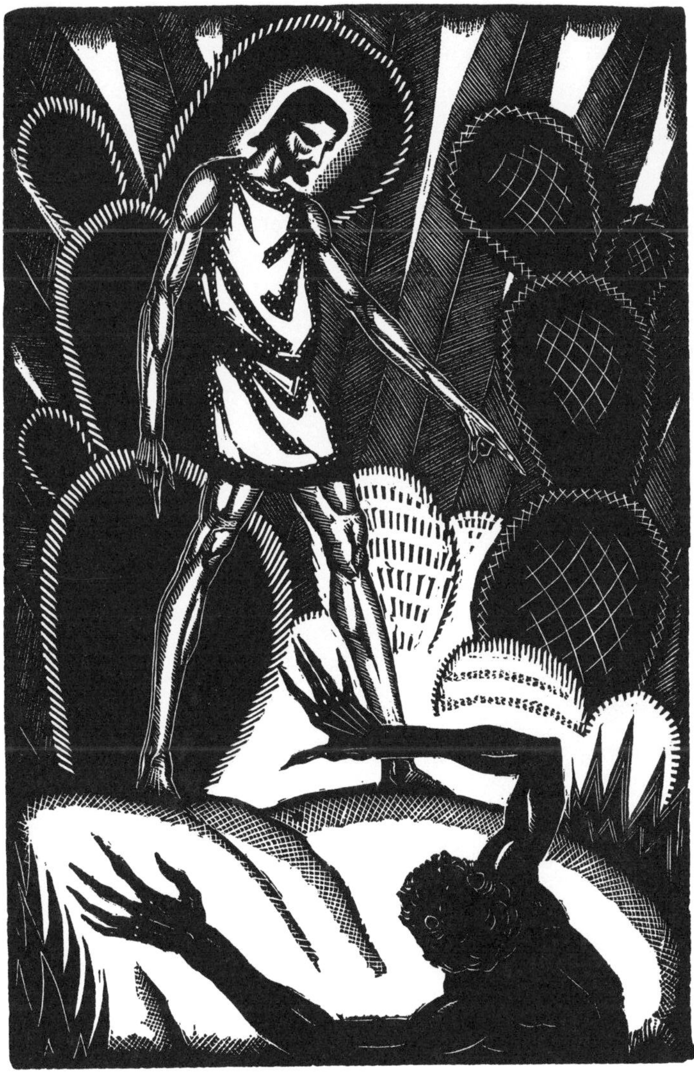

THE SON OF MAN

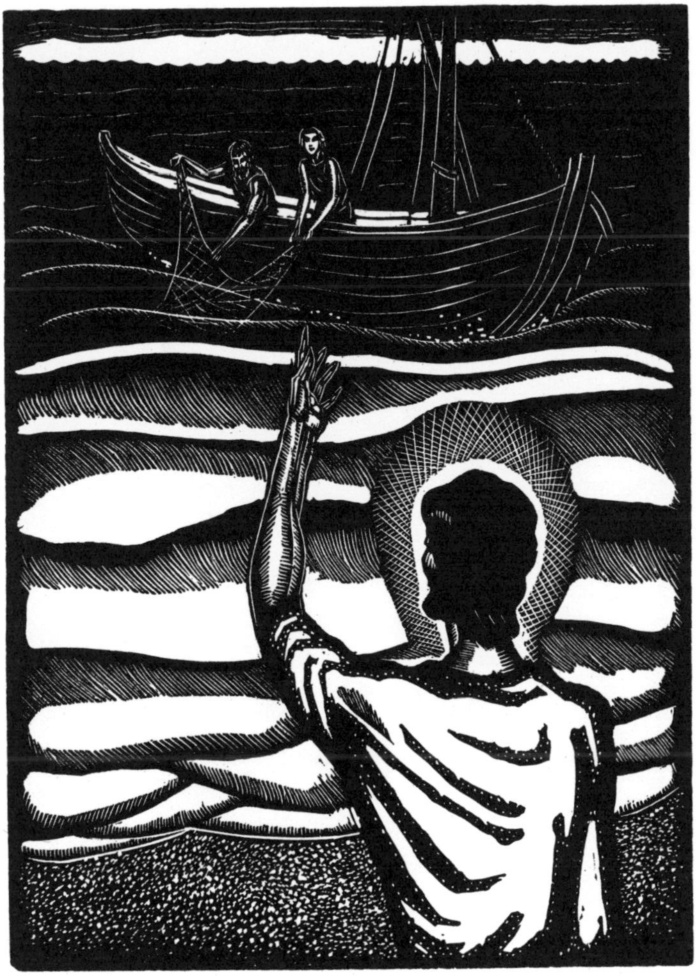

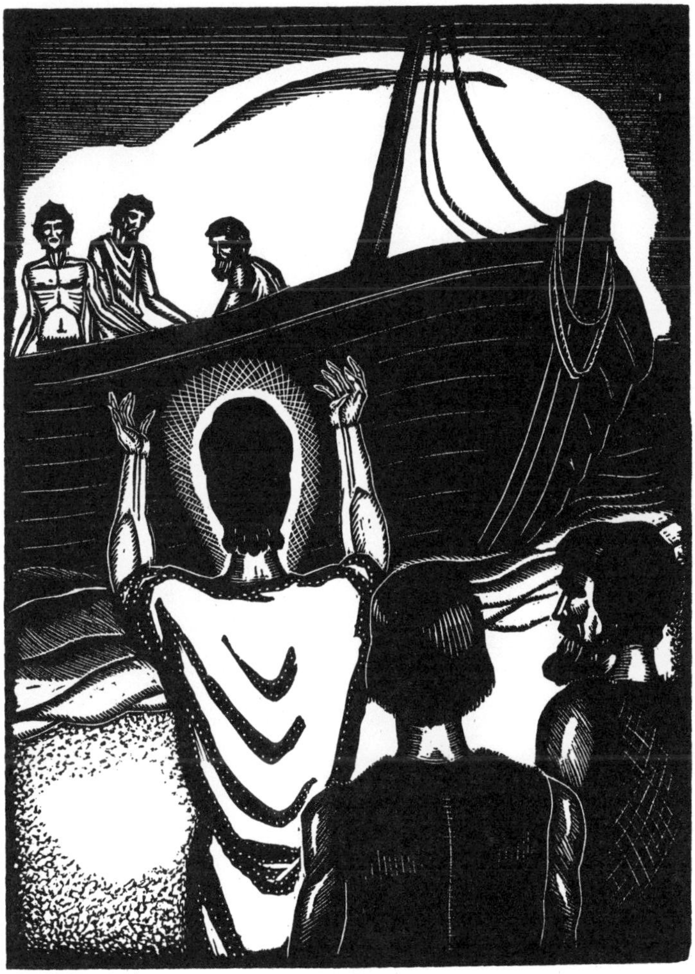

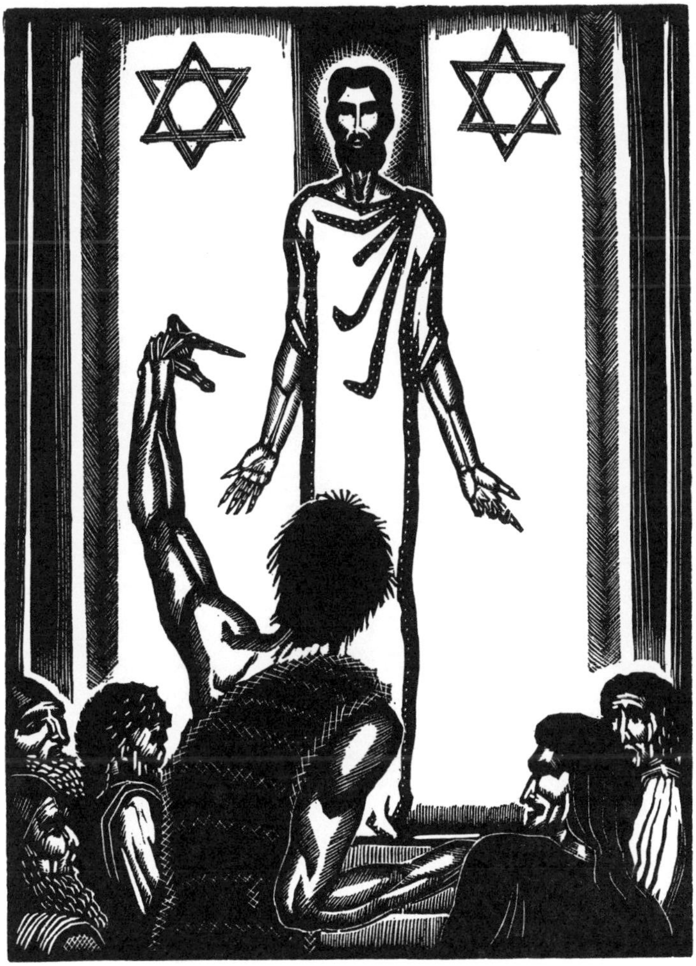

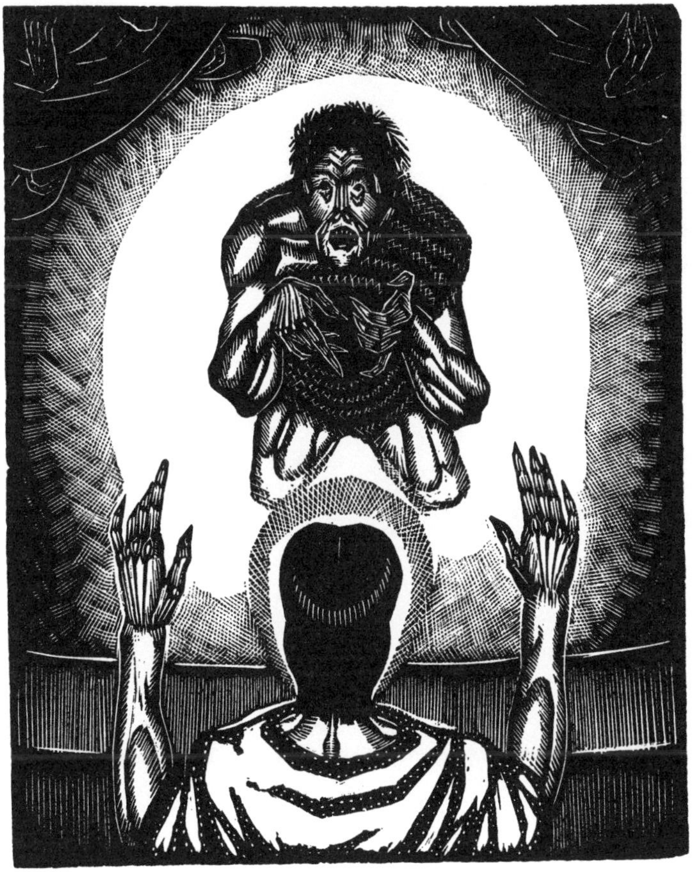

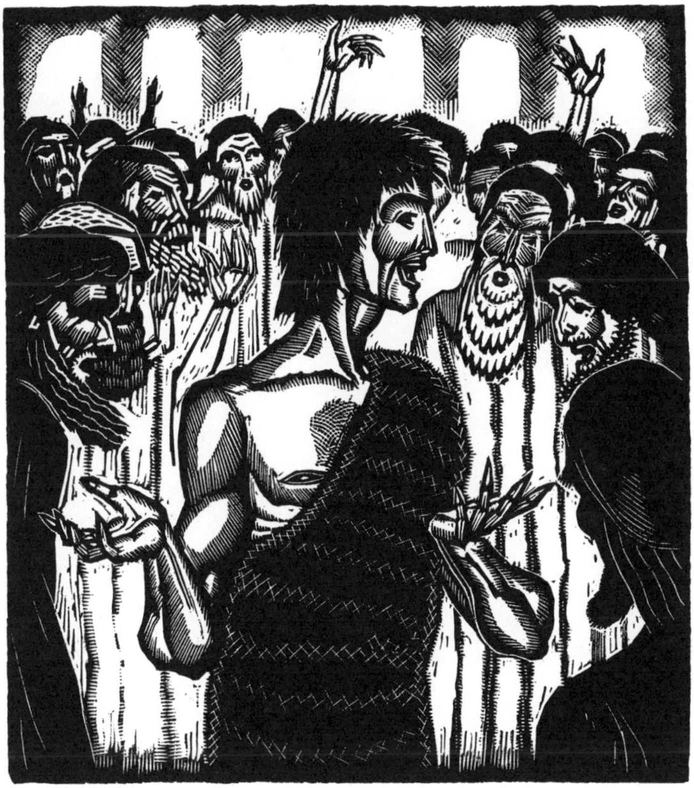

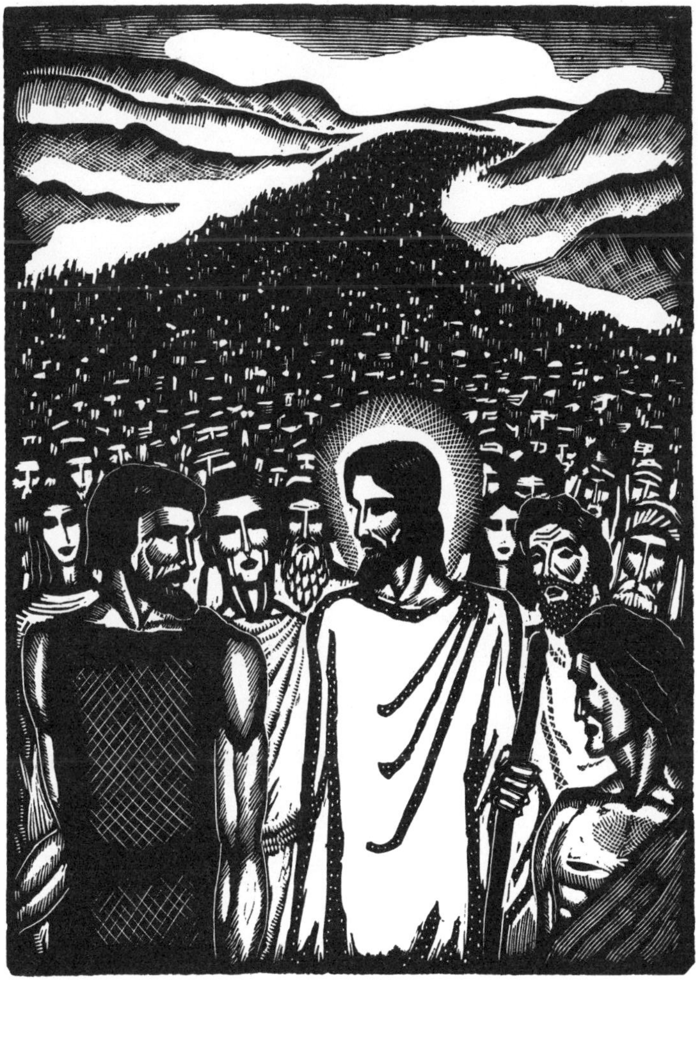

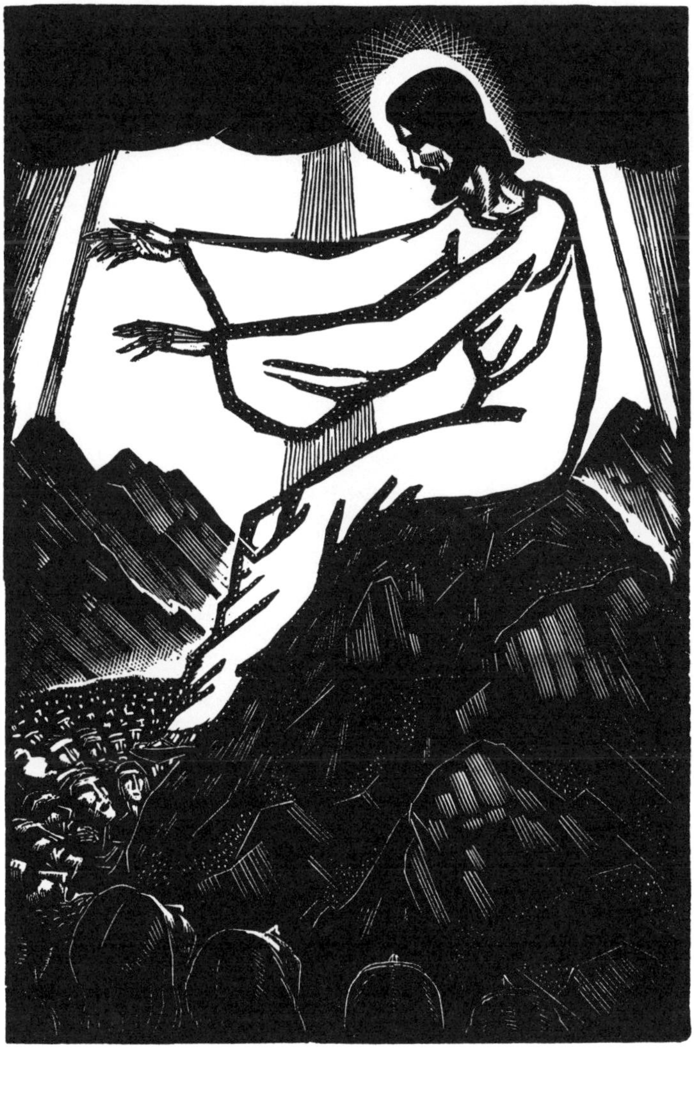

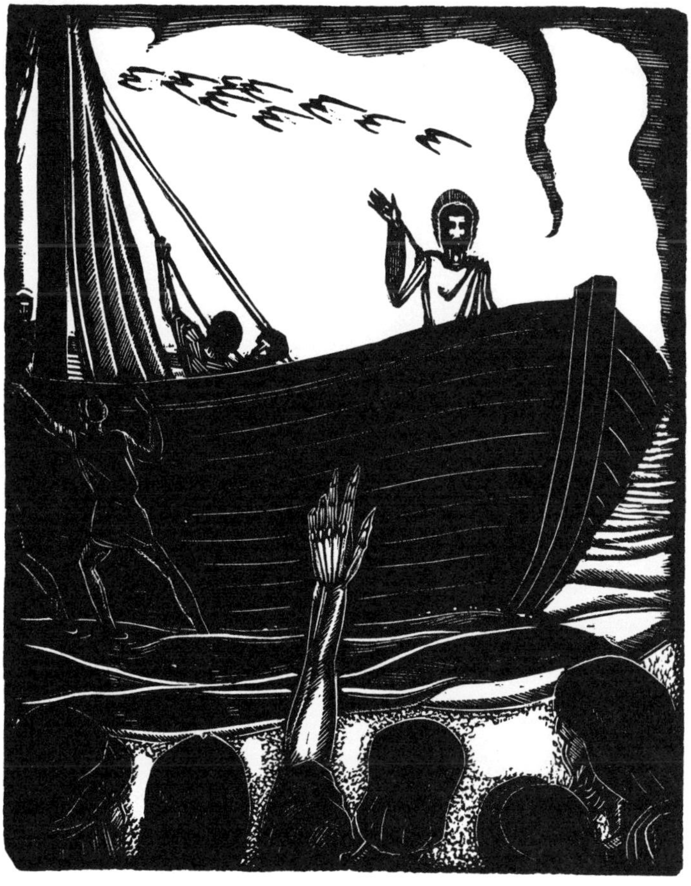

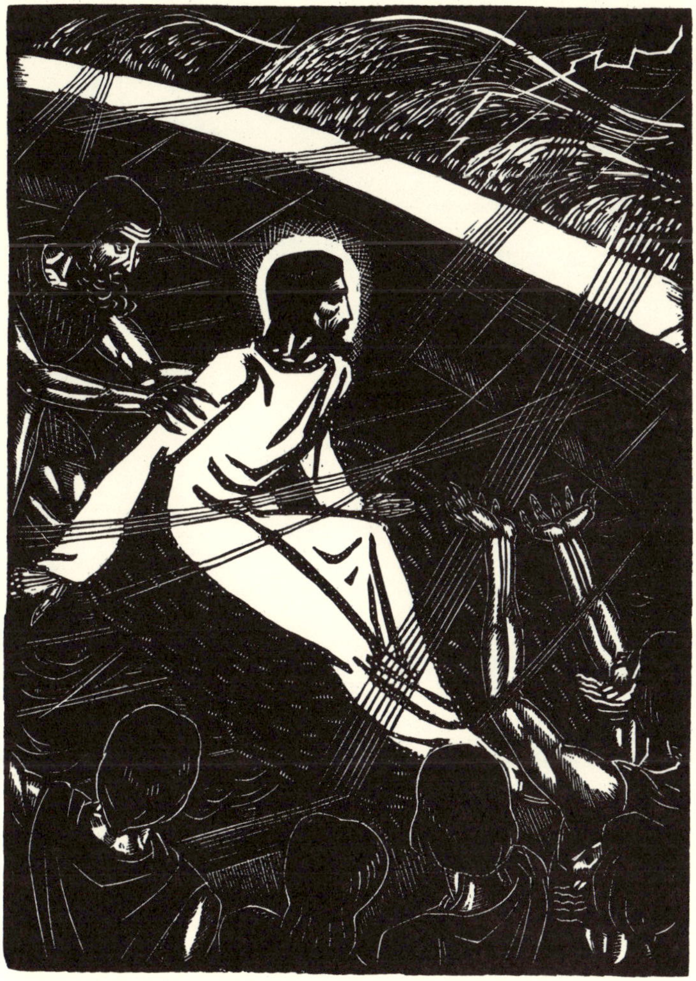

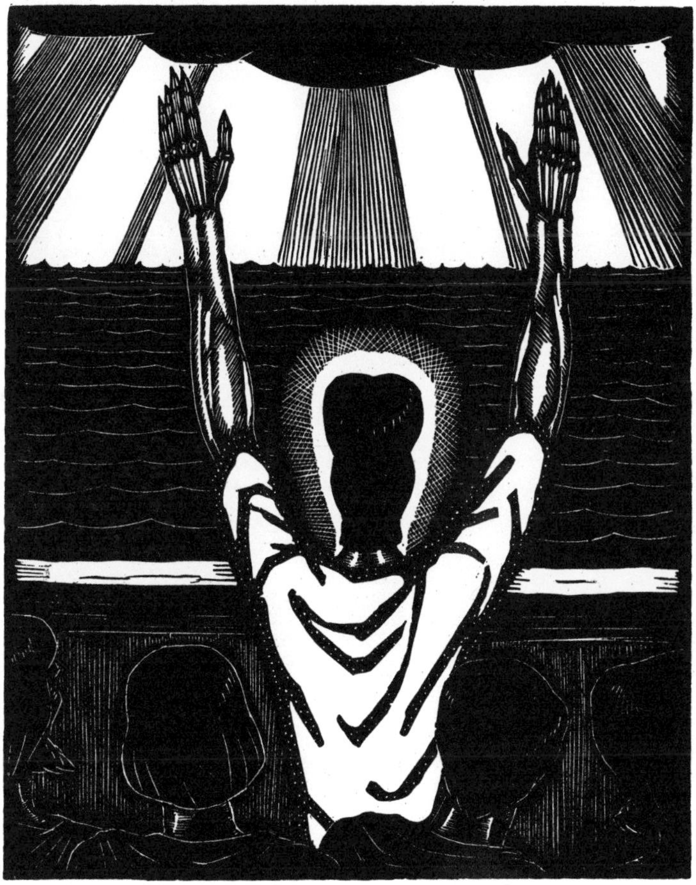

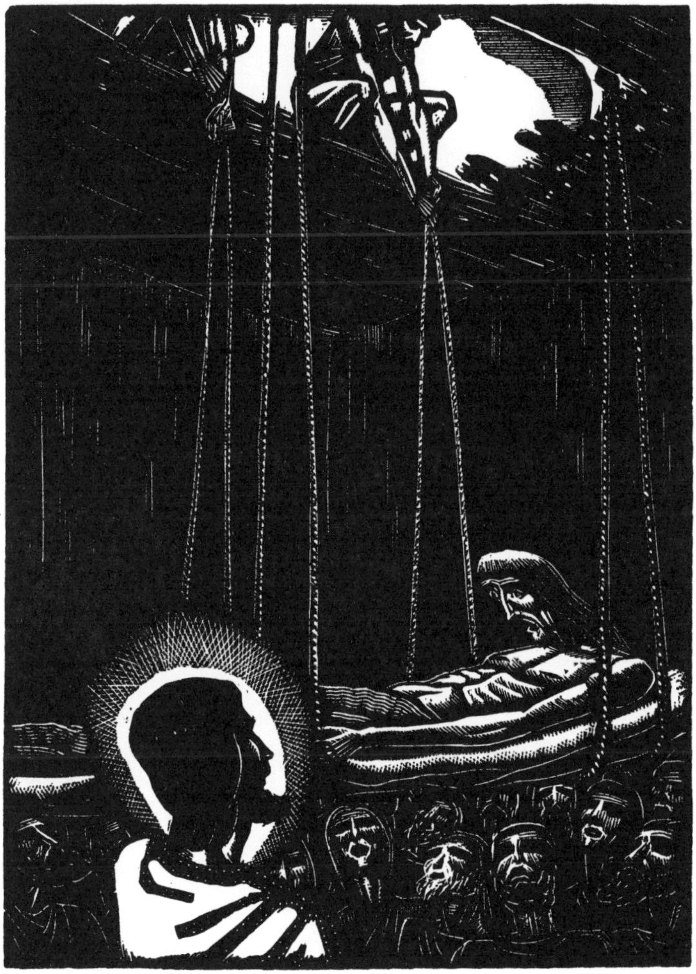

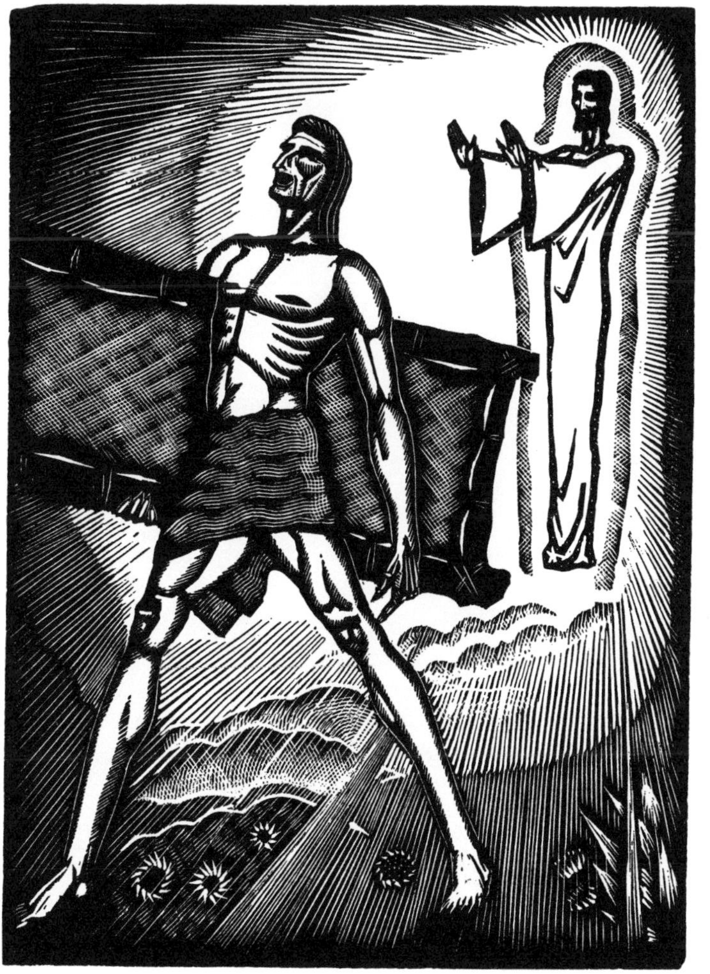

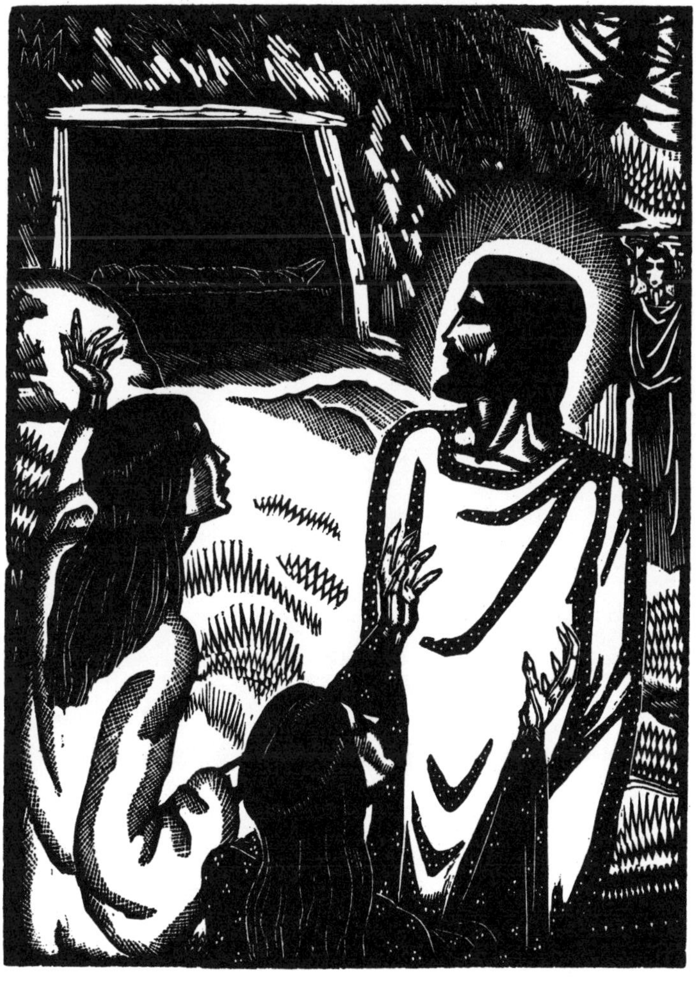

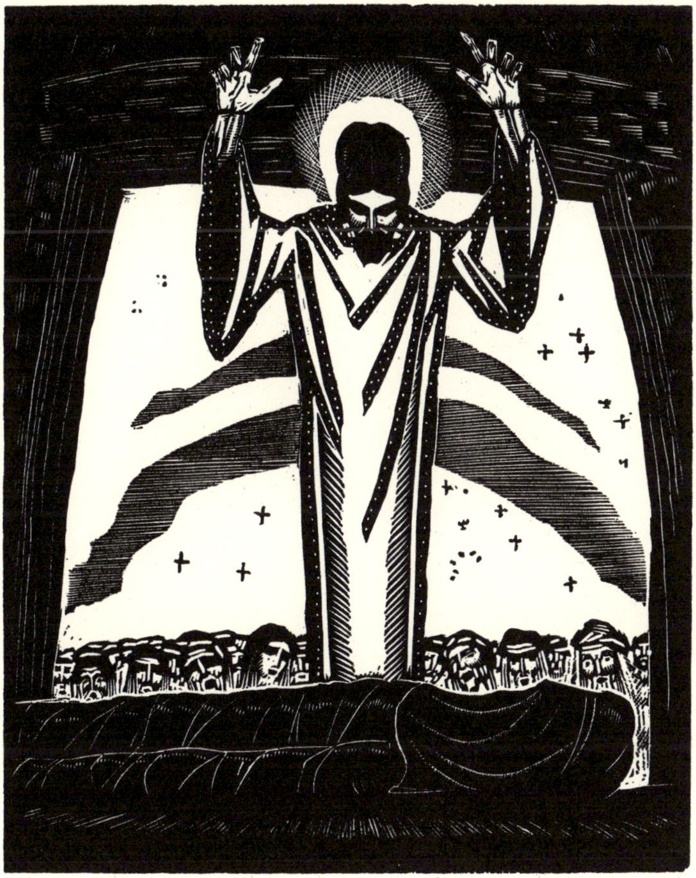

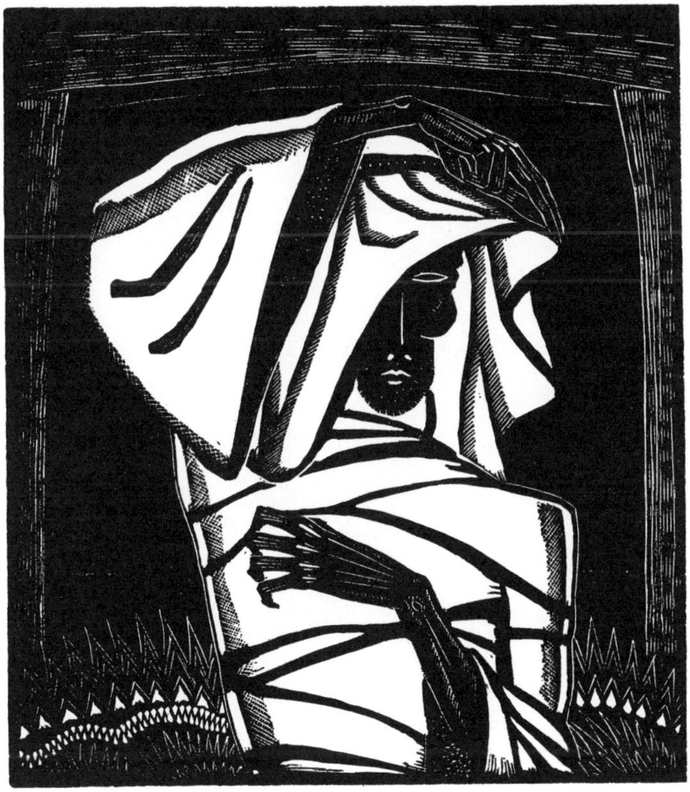

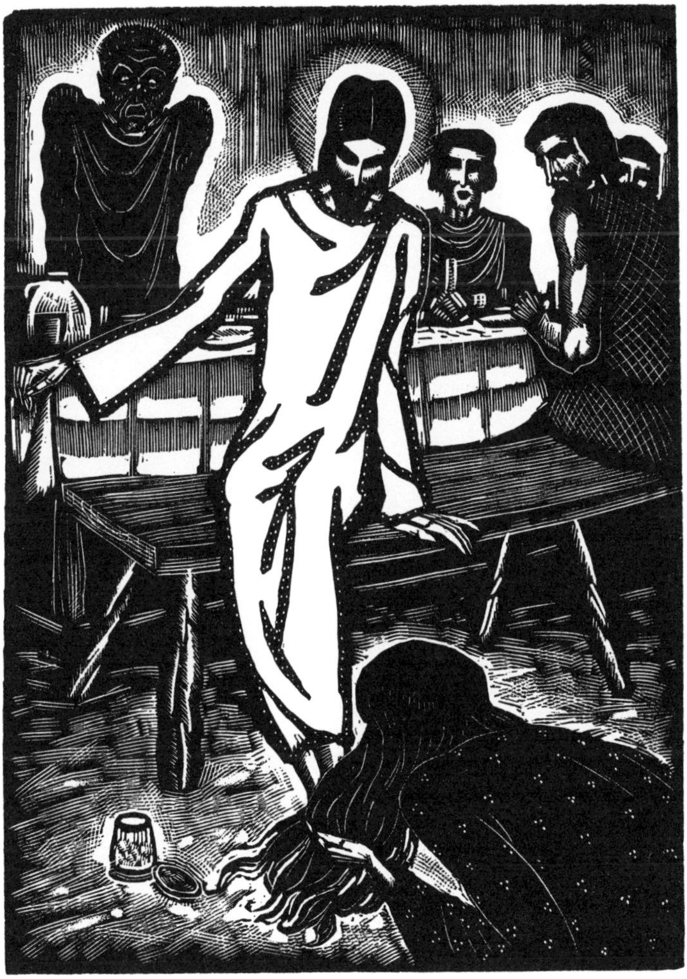

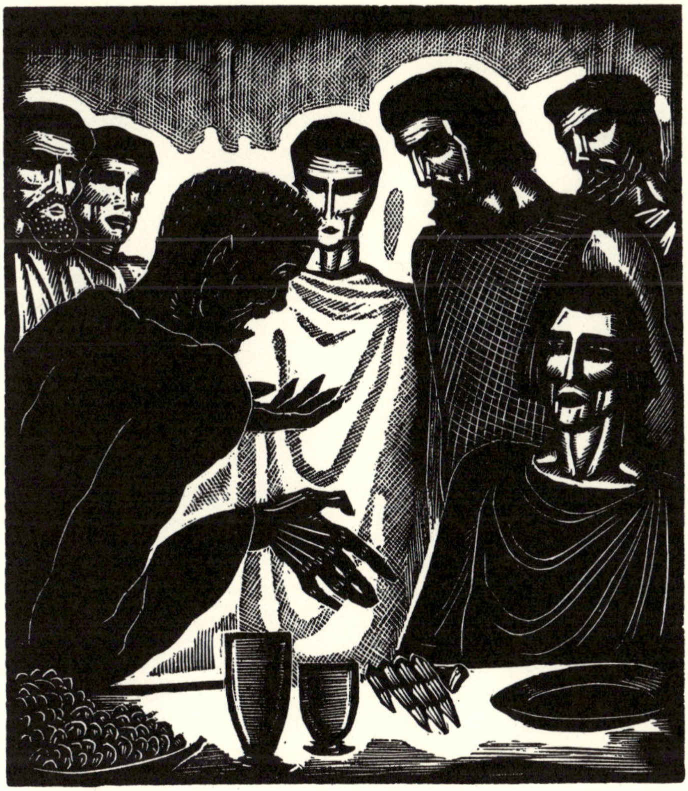

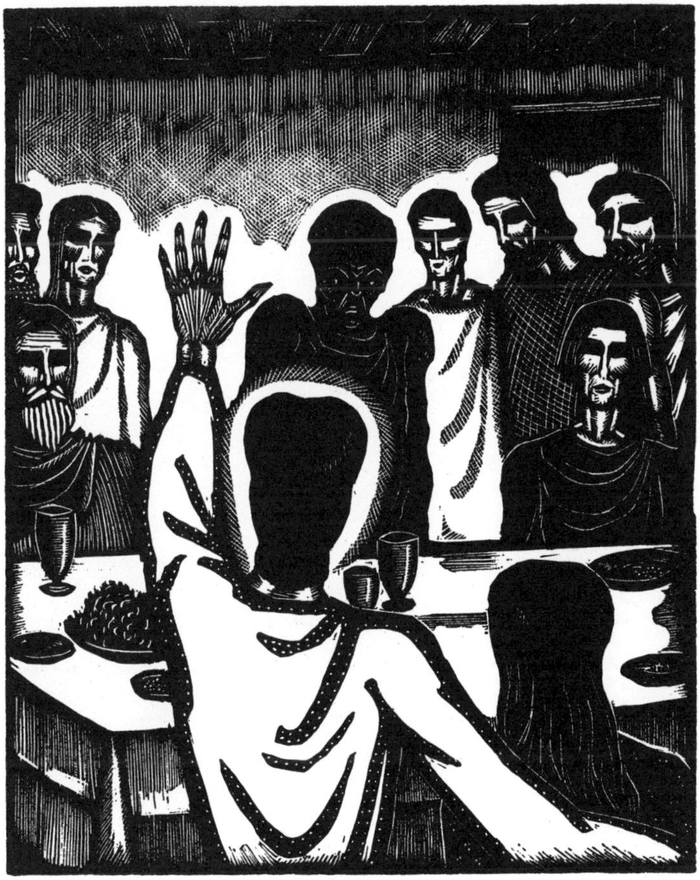

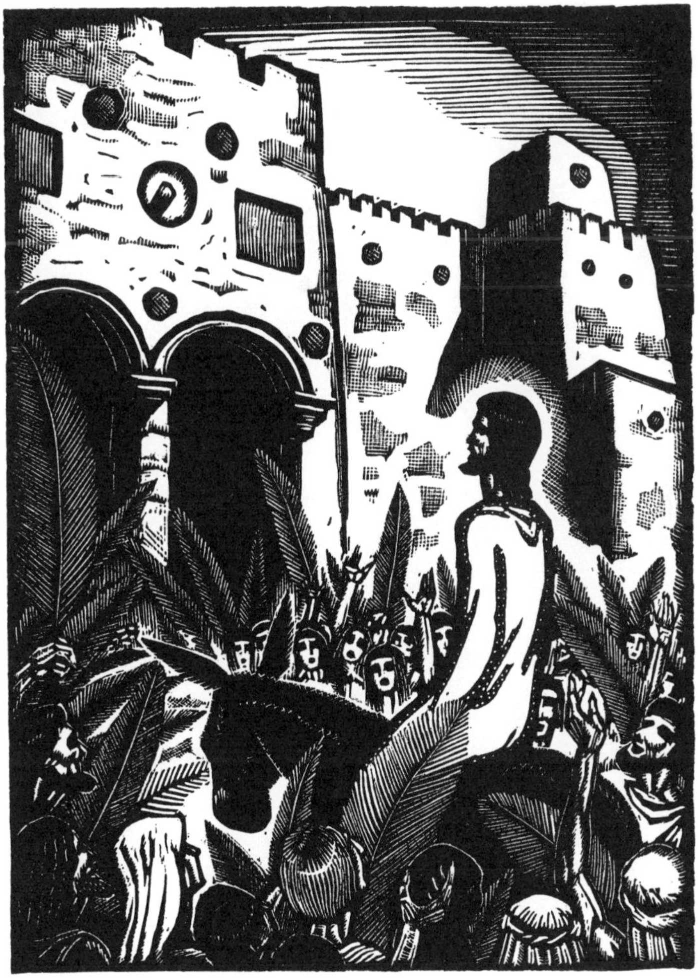

THE MESSIAH

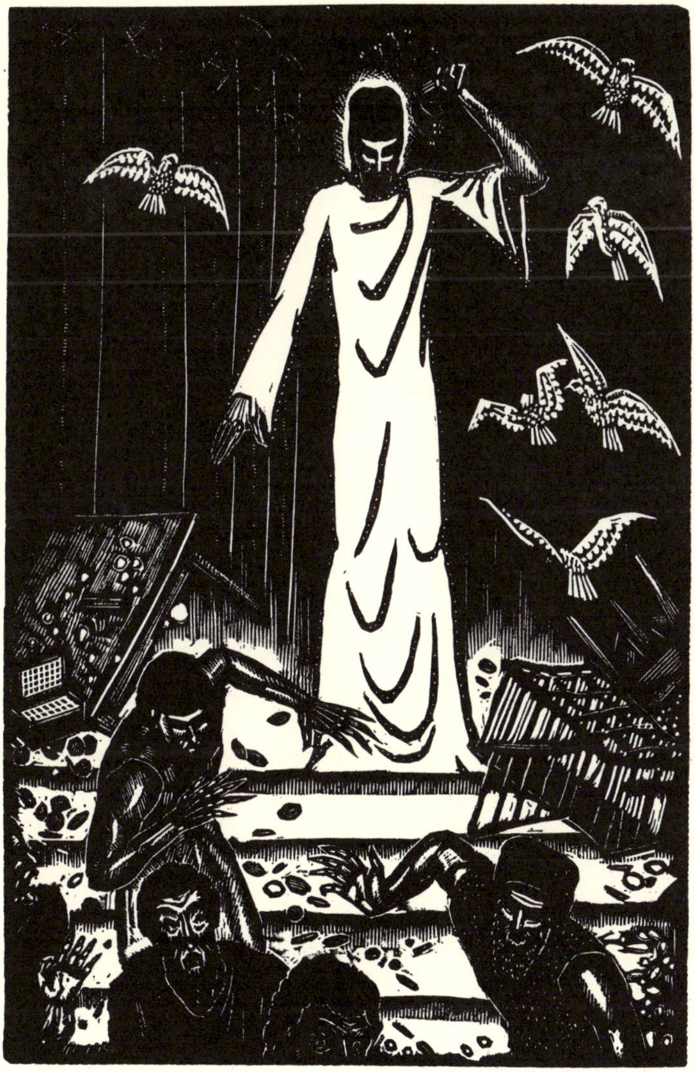

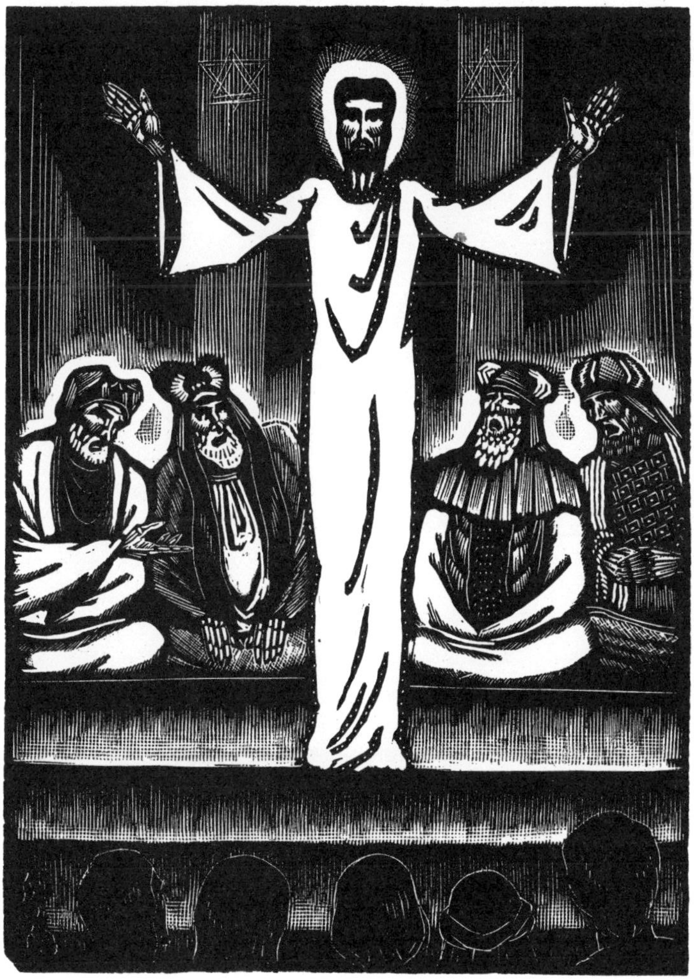

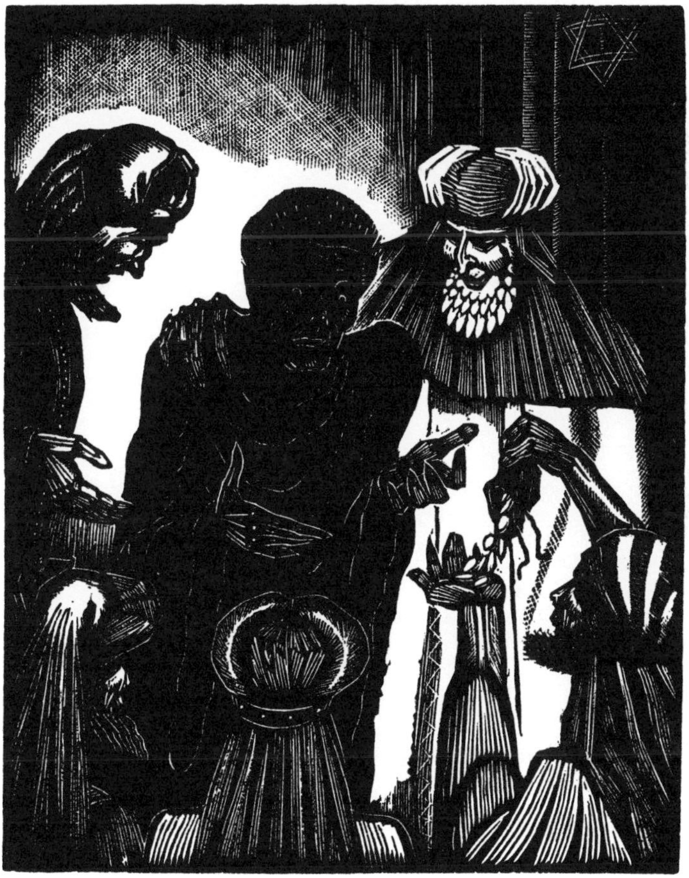

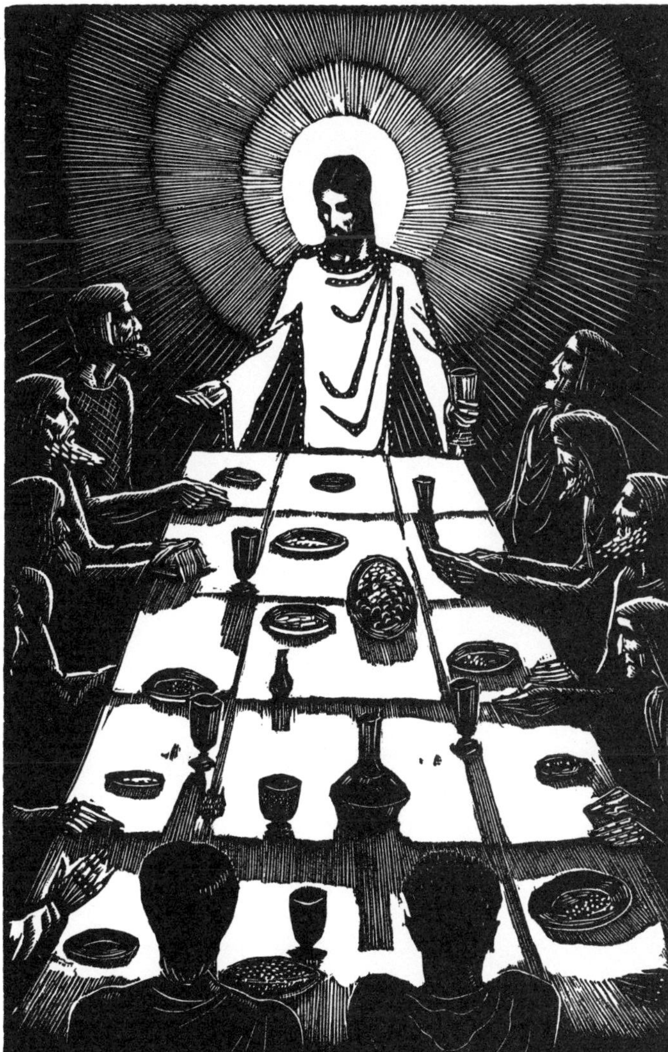

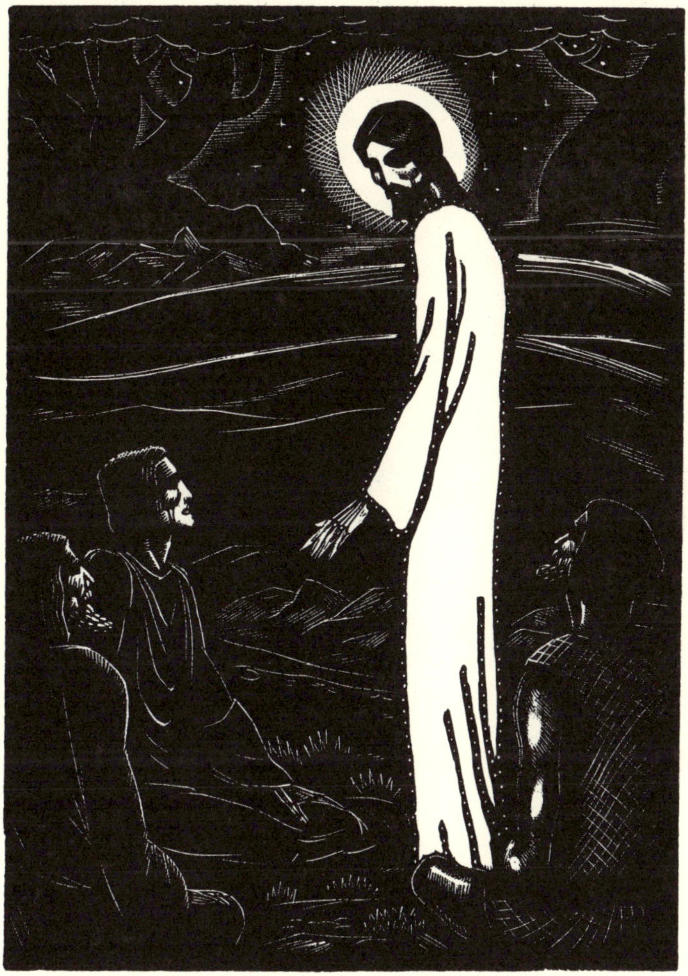

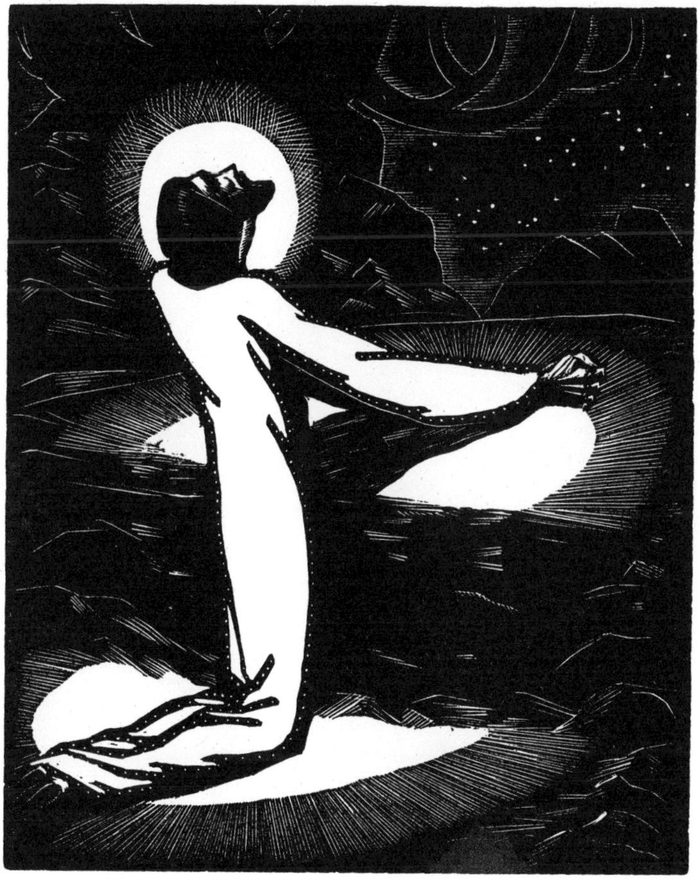

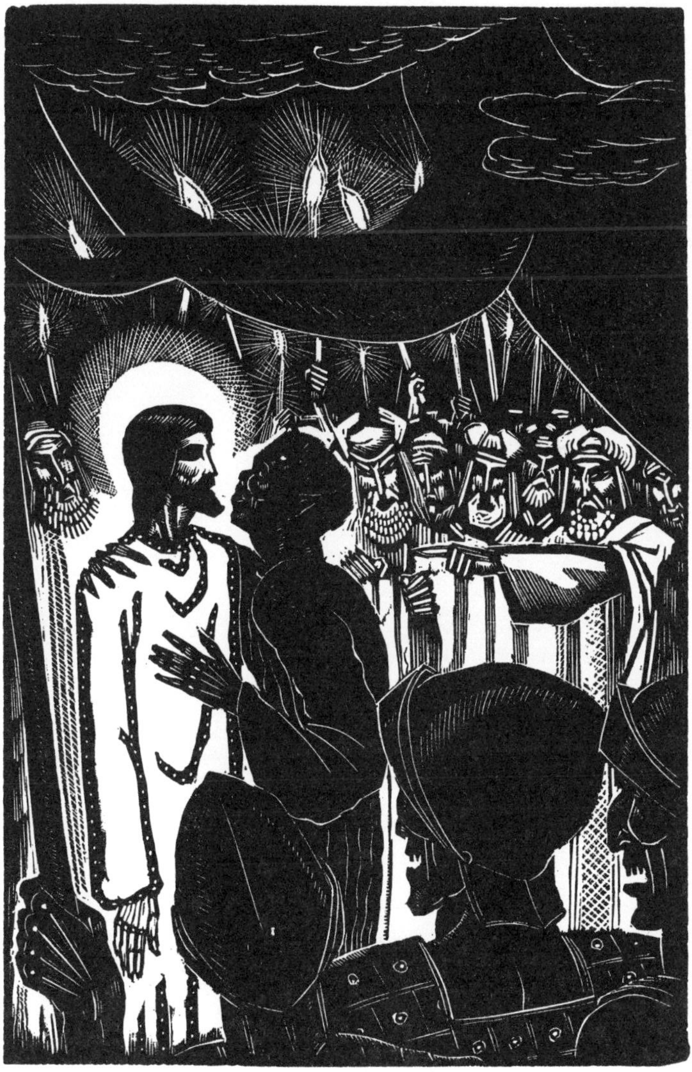

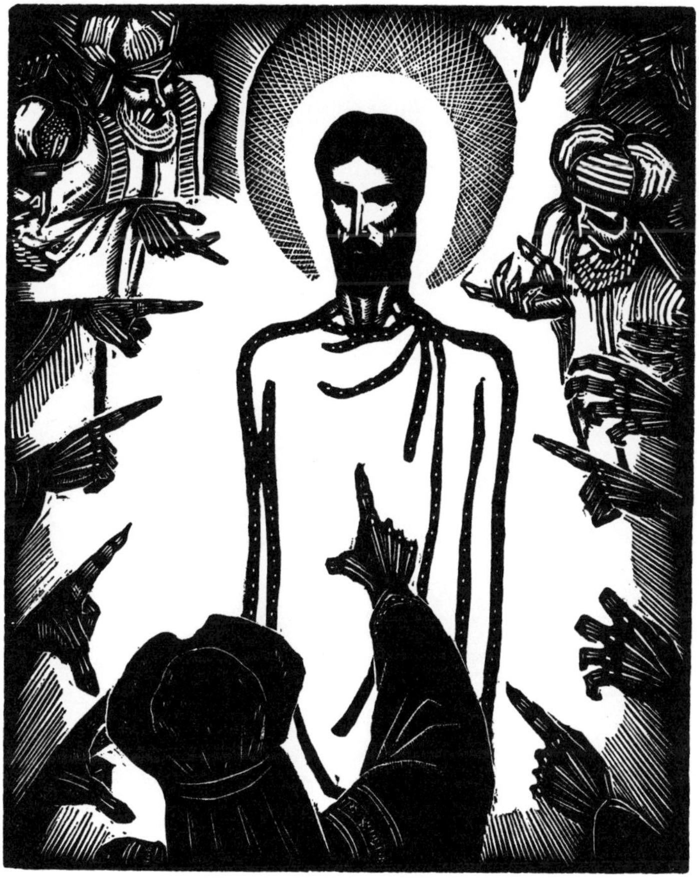

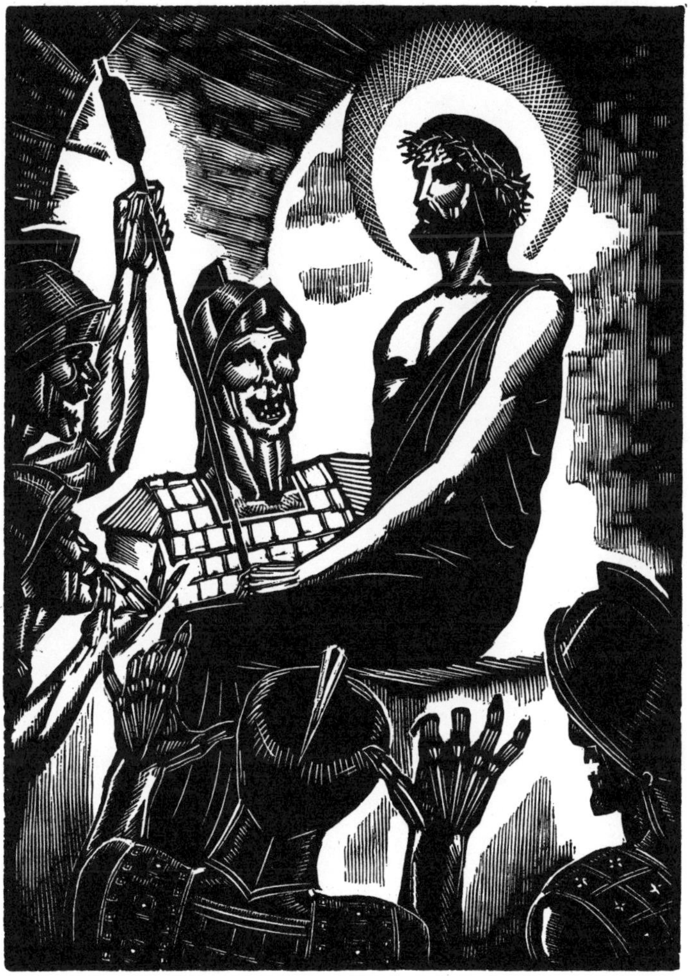

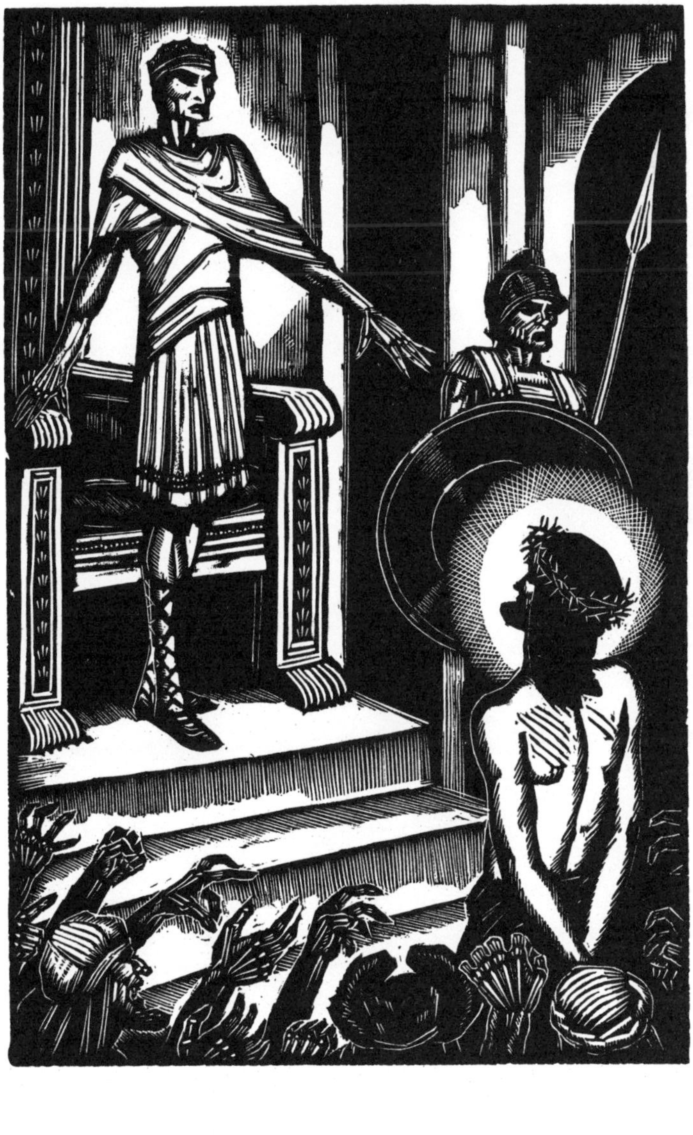

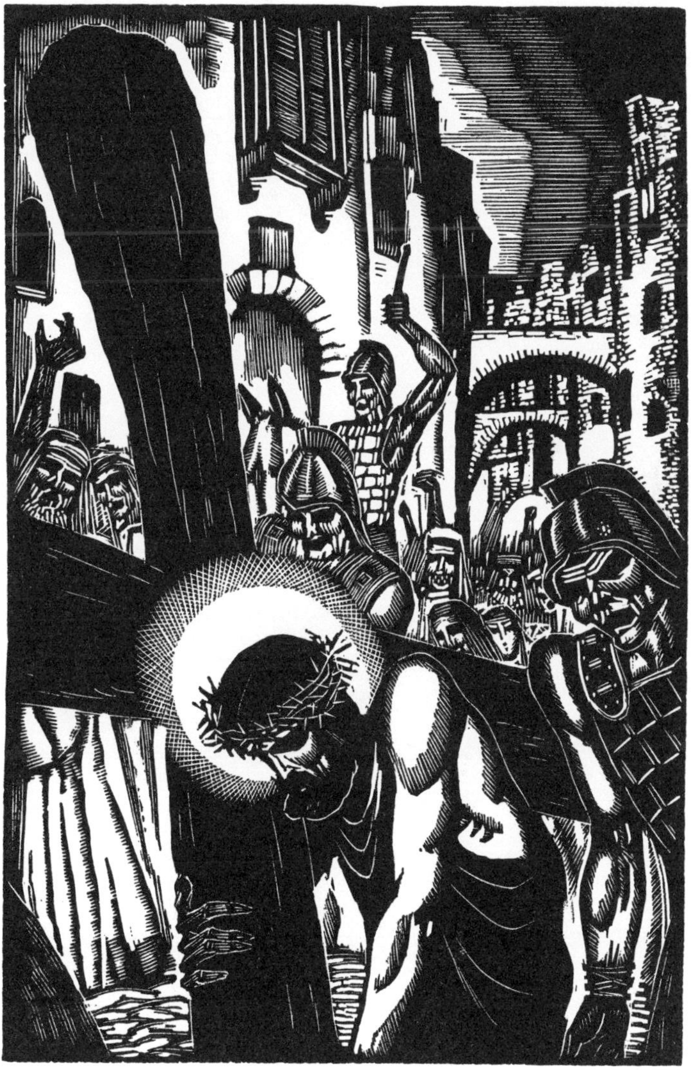

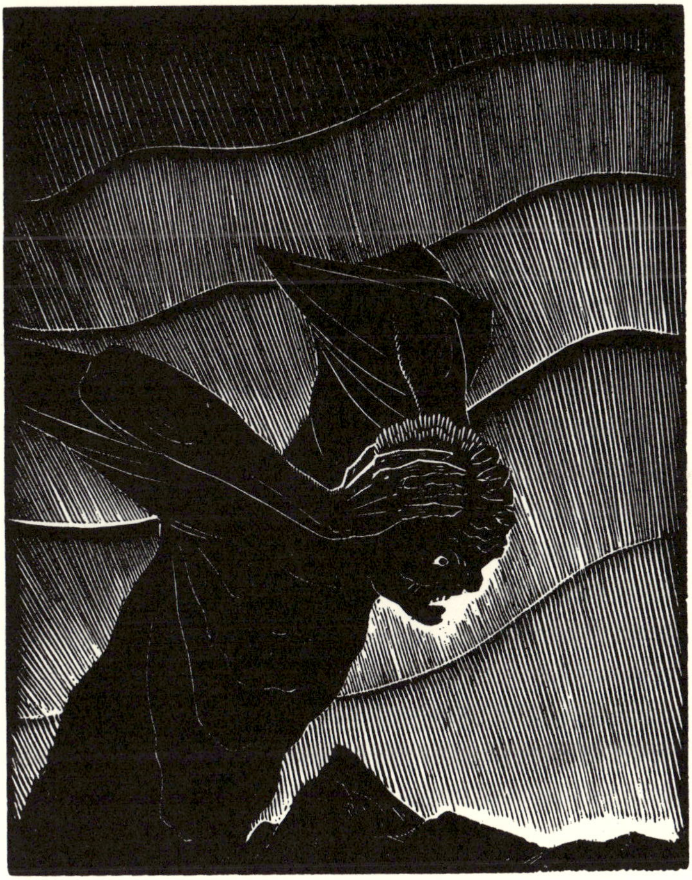

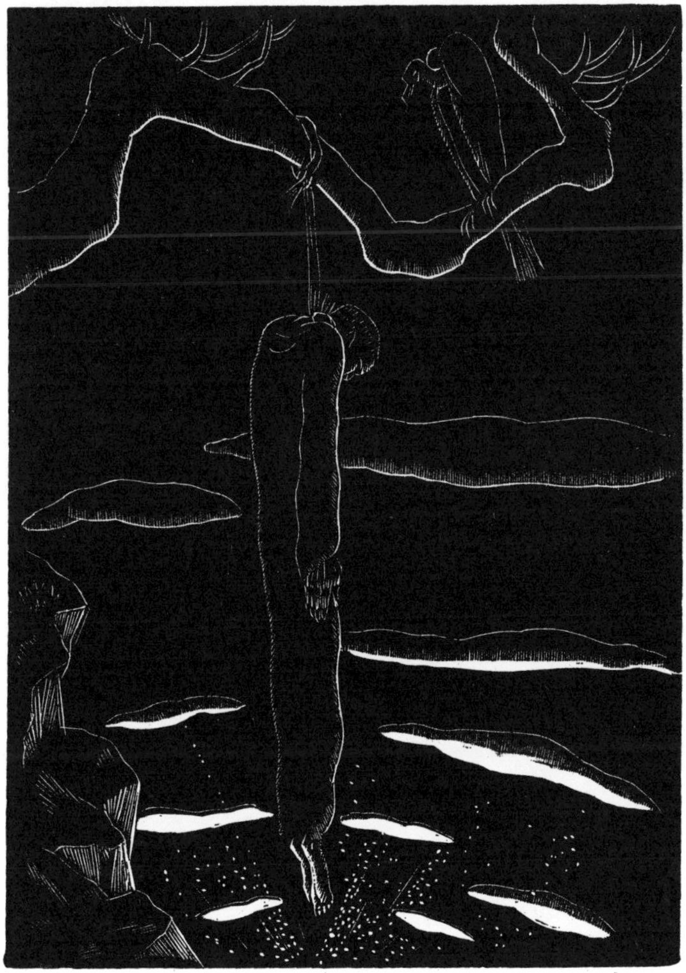

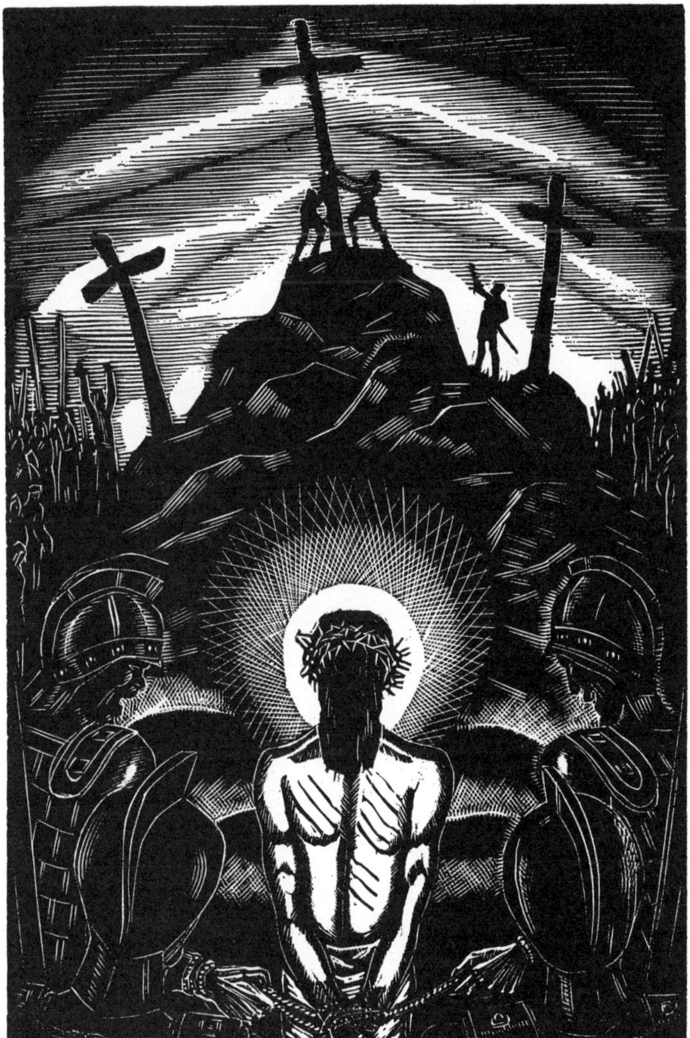

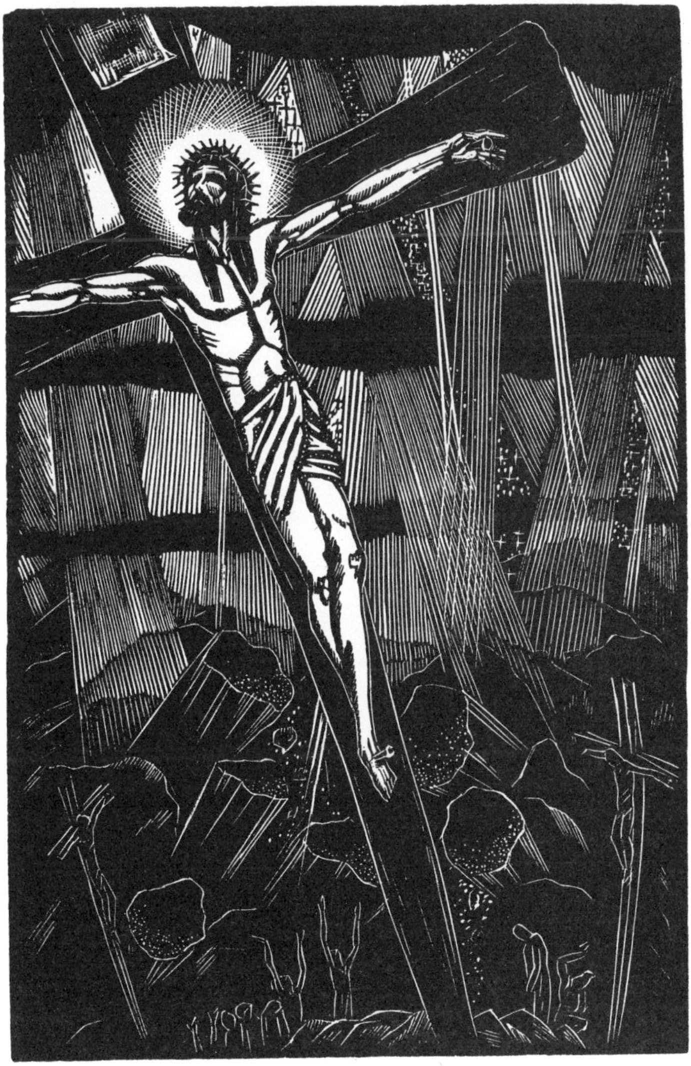

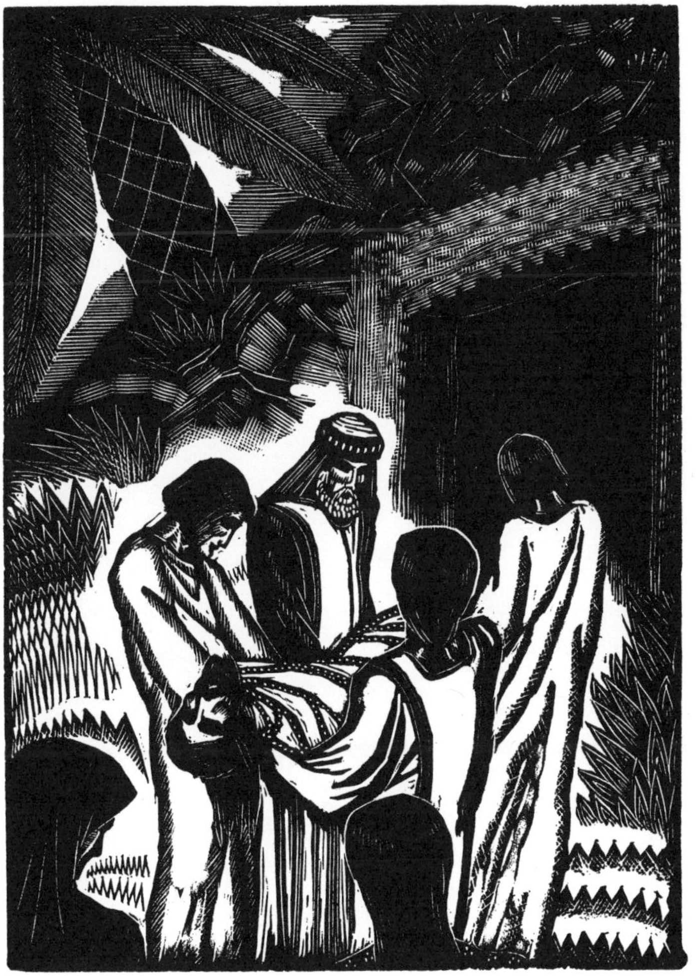

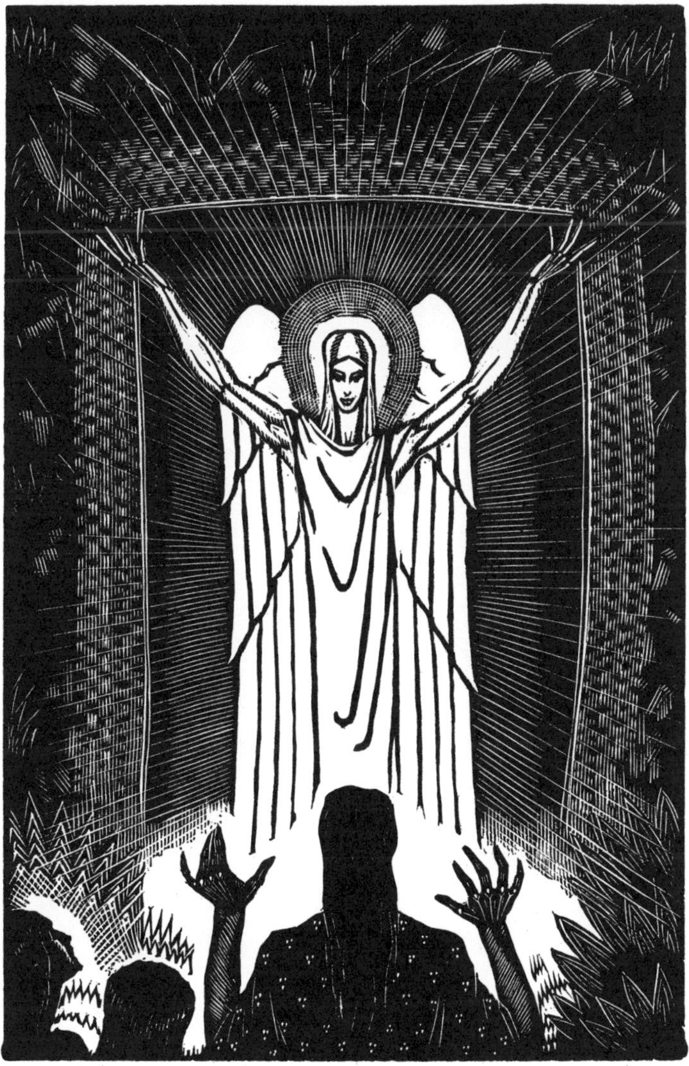

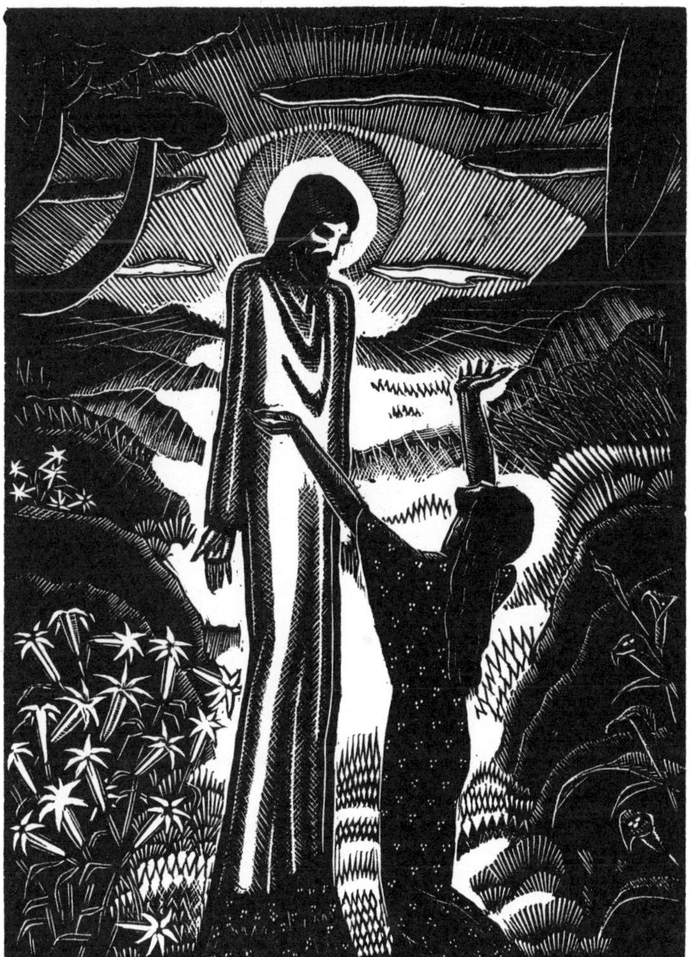

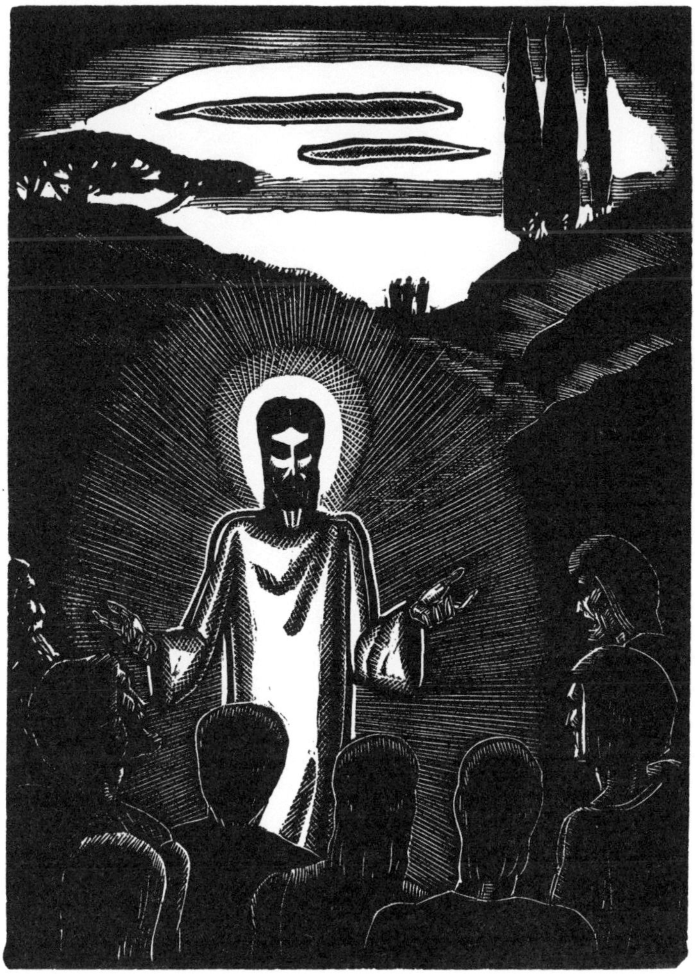

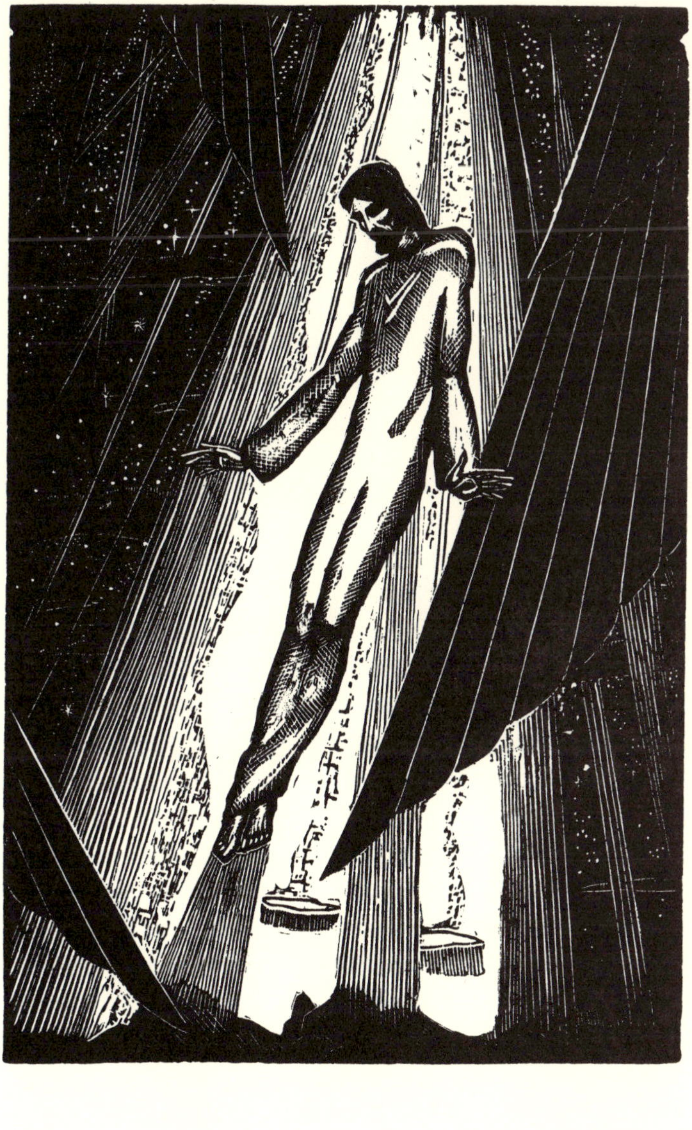

FINIS

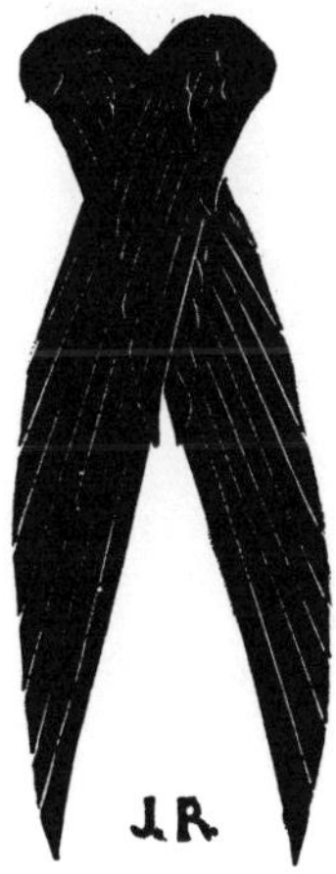